Great Depressions:
1837–1844, 1893–1898, 1929–1939

SCOTT FORESMAN PROBLEMS IN AMERICAN HISTORY

General Editors: **Edwin Fenton,** *Carnegie Institute of Technology*
David H. Fowler, *Carnegie Institute of Technology*

Volumes in this series:

THE CAUSES OF WAR:
The American Revolution, The Civil War, and World War 1
Kenyon C. Cramer

THE NEGRO IN AMERICA
Larry Cuban

LABOR IN AMERICAN SOCIETY
Raymond S. Iman and Thomas W. Koch

THE SUPREME COURT IN AMERICAN LIFE
Leonard F. James

AMERICAN FOREIGN POLICY
Leonard F. James

THE SOCIAL SETTING OF INTOLERANCE:
The Know-Nothings, The Red Scare, and McCarthyism
Seymour J. Mandelbaum

REFORM IN AMERICA:
Jacksonian Democracy, Progressivism, and The New Deal
Faye Rattner

GREAT DEPRESSIONS:
1837–1844, 1893–1898, 1929–1939
John Sperling

POLITICAL LEADERSHIP IN AMERICA
Emmett Wright, Jr.

Great Depressions:

1837-1844, 1893-1898, 1929-1939

John Sperling, *Associate Professor of History,*
San Jose State College, San Jose, California

SCOTT, FORESMAN AND COMPANY

Chicago • Atlanta • Dallas • Palo Alto • Fair Lawn, N.J.

COVER DESIGN BY ED BEDNO

Editors' Introduction

Growing numbers of history teachers realize that using source materials in their courses provides an added dimension of experience for their students. Total reliance on a textbook can no longer be considered an adequate means of learning history. Yet if the full value of documents and critical articles is to be obtained, they must be presented as something more than writings which record important events or as mere illustrations of what the text says. They must also challenge the student's ability to relate individual events to larger topics and to continuing themes in history.

Each volume of the SCOTT FORESMAN PROBLEMS IN AMERICAN HISTORY organizes source materials around one facet of our nation's past. A volume contains fifteen Problems, each designed for one day's work. In some of the books the Problems are intended to be read individually, at the proper chronological intervals. In others, they are grouped into three units of five Problems each, such a unit being best used as an uninterrupted week's work. Whether the Problems are studied individually or in units, they should be assigned only after the student has read the relevant material in his textbook.

One of the most vital services a collection of source materials can perform is to encourage the student to develop his critical abilities to the utmost in constructing historical explanations. Interpretation is the heart of history; the student should be brought to realize how essential it is to be able to do more with facts than memorize them. The SCOTT FORESMAN PROBLEMS are specifically designed to engage the student in the fascinating task of interpreting American history. Through them he will gain the skills and the enjoyment which come from reaching insight and understanding as well as knowledge of history.

Each Problem begins with an introduction written by the author to place documents in their historical context and to link together the Problems in a volume. These introductions prepare the student to read intelligently by defining the scope of the Problem, suggesting its relationship to larger issues, and pointing out difficulties of interpretation so that he will not attempt the impossible in generalizing from limited evidence.

The study questions at the end of the introduction carry the student further in applying the historian's critical tools. He may be asked to try to judge the reliability of a document or the bias of a critic, to assess an historical interpretation in the light of his knowledge, or to reason from particulars to a general conclusion of his own. Properly used, the study questions help beginning students find out what is important in source materials; without them, students often do not know what they are supposed to do with the readings.

To obtain more from a Problem than simply answers to the author's questions, the student should first read the introduction and questions and then pause to review what he already knows about the subject. Then, keeping the central issues in mind, he should study the entire Problem, perhaps first skimming through it to see the relationship of the parts to the whole, and then reading it carefully and taking notes. He will then be ready to consider his answers to the study questions in preparation for class discussion.

The teacher can use the SCOTT FORESMAN PROBLEMS in several ways. A Problem can perhaps serve most effectively as the basis for discussion by an entire class, with the lesson organized around the study questions or other questions proposed by the teacher to develop new points of view. What seems most appropriate for discussion will always depend partly upon the textbook used in the course and partly upon the instructor's own style of teaching and command of the subject. Each teacher should structure the discussion around those issues which he thinks are most important, but he should take care to link a Problem to those which precede and which follow it. These connecting links give the student the maximum opportunity to comprehend the theme of the volume. By treating a limited number of issues within each Problem, a teacher should be able to restrict discussion to one class period.

These volumes can be used in other ways. Many readings can serve as the basis for reports to the class by individual students. An entire volume, or a selection of Problems from a volume, may be used in preparing a controlled research paper; the three-unit volumes are especially suited to this purpose. The Problems may also be assigned as supplementary reading in those areas where text treatment is not extensive.

In *Great Depressions* Professor John Sperling explores one of the most significant aspects of American economic history. The readings examine the causes and the effects of three of the most dramatic depressions experienced by the nation. The final reading in each of the units provides an interpretation of the particular depression by an authority in the field. Students who use this volume are certain to gain fresh insights into three vital periods of American economic history and to discover new tools of economic analysis which will prove useful for the study of depressions generally.

EDWIN FENTON
DAVID H. FOWLER

PUBLISHER'S NOTE: The readings in this volume show capitalization and spelling of words, as well as sentence punctuation, as they appear in the sources from which they were taken. Thus, although the Problem introductions and headnotes are according to Scott, Foresman and Company editorial style, many of the readings are not. Omissions from the original texts are shown by ellipses, and interpolations, supplied by the author or editors for clarity, appear in brackets.

Table of Contents

Author's Introduction

Depressions, like wars and revolutions, fascinate students of history. The reasons are not hard to find. A depression places society under stress, and stress reveals much which is not always apparent during normal times about the way a society operates. A depression also prompts people to demand government action to soften the impact of hard times and to prevent a recurrence. Debates at times of depression over the nature of government policy reveal rival political, social, and economic philosophies. Finally, the problem of why depressions begin and end intrigues economists and historians.

The three most important depressions in United States history were separated widely in time. One lasted from 1837 to 1844, another from 1893 to 1898, and a third from 1929 to 1939. Each depression had a different origin, a different history, and a different effect, but all brought human suffering and intense political conflict.

The economy of a nation is its system of production and distribution of goods. A national economy includes in varying degrees a supply of natural resources, capital, a work force, and technology. During the years from 1837 to 1844, the economy in America was overwhelmingly agricultural. Since farmers could raise food for their families, physical distress during the depression was limited, but business activity shrank severely and economic growth slowed for a decade. A sharp political debate over the role of the second Bank of the United States had preceded this depression. During the course of the slump, this debate widened to include questions about the money and banking system, the issue of government-created monopolies, and the proper role of the federal government in the economy. By the time the depression ended, those who argued for uninhibited free enterprise had won the day. Their views were later ratified by the triumph of the industrial North in the Civil War.

By the 1890's America had industrialized. When depression struck in 1893, urban dwellers who lost their factory jobs rarely had farms of their own for a food supply. The unemployed suffered severely; many turned to private charities and to the government to fend off starvation. The sight of millions dependent on charity shocked many Americans. In times of prosperity the conflict between those who believed in self-reliance and others who advocated public responsibility for the unfortunate remained dormant. During bad times, however, it broke out in vigorous public debate. Unemployed millions could not be argued away in 1894. No amount of exhortation about self-reliance could feed them or provide new jobs. The tragedy of the depression forced many Americans to re-evaluate their fundamental economic philosophy.

Some state and local governments acted to provide relief for the people under their jurisdiction, but in Washington, the President—whether the incumbent was a Democrat or a Republican—clung to self-help as the solution. Consequently, millions of resentful farmers, joined by some city workers, stirred up great political revolt in the Populist crusade. Although the movement collapsed in the campaign of 1896, the Populists focused widespread attention on the problems of industrialization and unemployment. The Progressive movement grew out of this concern.

The depression that began in 1929 further weakened American faith in rugged individualism as the political basis for a modern industrial economy. Beginning with Franklin D. Roosevelt, each President initiated or supported massive programs involving government action to maintain prosperity and provide economic security. The American people, accepting a new relationship between their government and their economic system, adopted an attitude toward possible solutions to economic depressions quite different from that of the nineteenth century.

JOHN SPERLING

unit one

The Depression of 1837-1844

In the middle third of the nineteenth century, Americans still lived in an agricultural society. At the same time they were caught up in a pell-mell race to move west, to industrialize, and to connect all sections of the country by transportation systems. Opportunity seemed endless and its variety encouraged a buoyant, speculative spirit. Vast reaches of virgin soil stretched out before the oxen which pulled covered wagons westward. In the East new mills dotted the river banks, and fortunes were to be made in trade with Europe. Similar fortunes lay waiting for the enterprising men who could link East and West with canals, turnpikes, and railroads.

Economically, the nation was composed of three major sections, each one with different characteristics and somewhat different problems. The South, increasingly dependent on cotton, wagered its prosperity on the price of its major cash crop. The Northwest, with the greatest proportion of subsistence farming, was also a prime source of grain and meat for the South, the Northeast, and Europe. The Northeast turned increasingly to manufacturing, to produce in the United States goods which had long been imported from across the Atlantic.

A number of economic ties bound the three sections of the country together. A substantial internal trade had developed. In addition the sections were tied together by a financial system organized primarily around private banks chartered by the states. Government policies concerning the tariff, the monetary system, the sales of western lands, and similar economic matters affected all sections. With these mutual concerns, the sections seemed likely to prosper or to suffer together.

In the Panic of 1837 and the seven years of hardship that followed, all sections did suffer, although some areas were harder hit than others. The five Problems in Unit One explore and analyze the train of events which produced the depression. Problem 1 examines the conflict over the Bank of the United States and the private banks chartered by the states. Problem 2 explores the nature of the boom in the early and middle 1830's. Problem 3 describes the panic that followed, and Problem 4 is concerned with the economy during the early years of the depression. Problem 5 presents three interpretations of the causes and effects of the depression of the early 1840's.

PROBLEM 1

The War Against the Bank

In the early years of the nineteenth century the federal government left the regulation of the supply of money to private banks. Money has three major economic functions. It serves as a medium by which men exchange one kind of goods for another. It also serves as a standard against which the value of goods can be measured. Finally, money not spent but accumulated acts as a "store of value"; that is, it serves as a *claim* on real wealth, exchangeable at any time for goods or services.

Under the Coinage Law of 1792, the United States mint could coin gold and silver for money, but both metals were so scarce that few coins were circulated. The Constitution forbade both the federal government and the states to issue paper money directly. The system of using checks (drafts against demand deposits) as money had not yet developed. Hence, the public was forced to rely for its money on bank notes issued by private companies, usually banks operating under a charter. A bank note was a printed piece of paper bearing a promise to pay the stated value of the note in specie (gold or silver) on demand.

The federal government had chartered two United States banks. The first was established in 1791 with a twenty-year charter that expired in 1811; the second received a twenty-year charter in 1816. The states also chartered banks. By the 1830's hundreds of the state banks had issued notes varying widely in value, which circulated as money. If a bank had a poor reputation or was far away and not well known, people refused to accept its notes at the value printed on them. A merchant, for example, might give only four dollars worth of goods for a five-dollar note of an unknown or unsound bank (a procedure known as "discounting"), or even might refuse to accept the note.

States required the banks they chartered to back their currency with specie. A bank charter specified that a certain percentage of the face value of the notes printed must be held in reserve in the form of gold and silver. However, many banks issued notes well beyond the reserve requirement. A banker assumed that not everyone who held his notes would demand specie at the same time, and, in order to make money for himself, he often printed more notes than he could possibly back with specie in his vaults. The banker would print as many notes as a customer wanted to borrow; he, then, would lend them to the customer, charge him interest, and make a profit.

Sometimes confidence in a bank declined to the point where a large number of people demanded specie for bank notes. If the bank could not pay in specie, its notes quickly declined in value. Loss of confidence in the notes of any bank often preceded loss of confidence in the bank as a place to do business; if depositors and other creditors withdrew their support, failure was inevitable. Widespread failures could disrupt the entire economic system.

Nicholas Biddle, as president of the second Bank of the United States (or BUS), tried to regulate this chaotic system. Because it conducted the financial business of the federal government, all federal funds were deposited in the BUS. As a result, it had the greatest financial resources in the banking community with branches across the nation. When the BUS received deposits in the form of private bank notes, it often demanded specie from the private banks in exchange. This practice reduced the reserves of specie in private bank vaults and, therefore, the amount of currency or bank notes which bankers could legally place in circulation. Both private banks and their customers became enemies of the BUS because its anti-inflationary policies restricted loans and raised interest rates.

Most Jacksonians opposed the Bank; the Whigs generally supported it. These forces came into direct conflict when the Whigs, for political reasons, proposed a new charter for the BUS well before 1836, when the second charter was to expire. The readings in Problem 1 illustrate the arguments over the issue of recharter. As you read them, think about the following questions:

1 What are the major arguments in favor of the Bank? against it? Are the arguments about the Bank mainly economic in nature? political? social?

2 Judging from these readings, who would benefit most if the Bank had won a new charter? in what ways? Who would benefit least?

3 How was the Bank related to the general economic prosperity?

4 How does the Benton selection show the sectional nature of the struggle?

I

THE FIRST BLOW

Within a year of his inauguration in 1829, President Jackson opened an attack on the second Bank of the United States. In his first annual message he questioned the constitutionality of the Bank and its effectiveness in maintaining a uniform and sound currency. ☐ James D. Richardson, Compiler, *Messages and Papers of the Presidents, 1789–1897*, Volume 2, p. 462. Washington, D.C.: Authority of Congress. Copyright © 1897 by James D. Richardson.

The charter of the Bank of the United States expires in 1836, and its stockholders will most probably apply for a renewal of their privileges. In order to avoid the evils resulting from precipitancy in a measure involving such important principles and such deep pecuniary interests, I feel that I can not, in justice to the parties interested, too soon present it to the deliberate consideration of the Legislature and the people. Both the constitutionality and the expediency of the law creating this bank are well questioned by a large portion of our fellow-citizens, and it must be admitted by all that it has failed in the great end of establishing a uniform and sound currency.

Under these circumstances, if such an institution is deemed essential to the fiscal operations of the Government, I submit to the wisdom of the Legislature whether a national one, founded upon the credit of the Government and its revenues, might not be devised which would avoid all constitutional difficulties and at the same time secure all the advantages to the Government and country that were expected to result from the present bank.

II

IN DEFENSE OF THE BANK

President Jackson's comments on the Bank were referred to the Ways and Means Committee of the House of Representatives. Although most of its members were Jacksonian Democrats, it issued a report which amounted to a defense of the Bank on constitutional and economic grounds. ☐ *The Report of the Committee of the House of Representatives,* 22nd Congress, 1st Session, Report Number 283, Volume 2, April 13, 1830, pp. 7–27. Washington, D.C.: United States Congress.

This brief history of the former and present bank forcibly suggests a few practical reflections. It is to be remarked, in the first place, that, since the adoption of the constitution, a bank has existed, under the authority of the Federal Government, for thirty-three out of forty years; during which time public and private credit has been maintained at an elevation fully equal to what has existed in any nation in the world: whereas, in the two short intervals, during which no national bank existed, public and private credit was greatly impaired, and, in the latter instance, the fiscal operations of the Government were almost entirely arrested. . . .

It must be assumed as the basis of all sound reasoning on this subject, that the existence of a paper currency, issued by banks deriving their charters from the State Governments, cannot be prohibited by Congress. . . .

But the question really presented for their [the committee's] determination is not between a metallic and a paper currency, but between a paper currency of uniform value, and subject to the control of the only power competent to its regulation, and a paper currency of varying and fluctuating value, and subject to no common or adequate control whatever. On this question it would seem that there could scarcely exist a difference of opinion; and that this is substantially the question involved in considering the expediency of a national bank, will satisfactorily appear by a comparison of the state of the currency previous to the establishment of the present bank, and its condition for the last ten years. . . .

For all the purposes of the revenue, it gives to the national currency that perfect uniformity, that ideal perfection, to which a currency of gold and silver, in so extensive a country, could have no pretensions. A bill issued at Missouri is of equal value with specie at Boston, in payment of duties; and the same is true of all other places, however distant, where the bank issues bills, and the Government collects its revenue. When it is, moreover, considered, that the bank performs, with the most scrupulous punctuality, the stipulation to transfer the funds of the Government to any point where they may be wanted, free of expense, it must be apparent that the committee are correct, to the very letter, in stating that the bank has furnished, both to the Government and to the people, *a currency of absolutely uniform value in all places, for all the purposes of paying the public contributions, and disbursing the public revenue.* . . .

But the salutary agency of the Bank of the United States, in furnishing a sound and uniform currency, is not confined to that portion of the currency which consists of its own bills. One of the most important purposes which the bank was designed to accomplish, and which, it is confidently believed, no other human agency could have effected, under our federative system of Government, was the enforcement of specie payments on the part of numerous local banks deriving their charters from the several States, and whose paper, irredeemable in specie, and illimitable in its quantity, constituted the almost entire currency of the country. Amidst a combination of the greatest difficulties, the bank has almost completely succeeded in the performance of this arduous, delicate, and painful duty. . . .

But the great injury which would result from the refusal of Congress to renew the charter of the present Bank, would, beyond all question, be that which would result to the community at large. . . . The Bank of the United States, in winding up its concerns, would not only withdraw its own paper from circulation, and call in its debts, but would unavoidably make such heavy draughts on the local institutions for specie, as very greatly to curtail their discounts. The pressure upon the active, industrious, and enterprising classes, who depend most on the facilities of bank credit, would be tremendous. A vast amount of property would change hands at half its value, passing under the hammer, from the merchants, manufacturers, and farmers, to the large moneyed capitalists, who always stand ready to avail themselves of the pecuniary embarrassments of the community.

III

VOICE OF THE DEMOCRACY

The Committee Report inspired speeches, pamphlets, and editorials on both sides of the issue. Senator Thomas Hart Benton of Missouri attacked the Bank and the use of paper money so vehemently in a number of speeches that his colleagues began to call him "Old Bullion." The following selection is from one of his Senate speeches delivered on February 2, 1831. ☐ Thomas Hart Benton, *Thirty Years' View,* Volume 1, pp. 191–193. New York: D. Appleton and Company, copyright © 1854.

First: Mr. President, I object to the renewal of the charter of the Bank of the United States, because I look upon the bank as an institution too great and powerful to be tolerated in a government of free and equal laws. Its power is that of the purse; a power more potent than that of the sword; and this power it possesses to a degree and extent that will enable this bank to draw to itself too much of the political power of this Union; and too much of the individual property of the citizens of these States. . . .

. . . The direct power of the bank is now prodigious, and in the event of the renewal of the charter must speedily become boundless and uncontrollable. The bank is now authorized to own effects, lands inclusive, to the amount of fifty-five millions of dollars, and to issue notes to the amount of thirty-five millions more. This makes ninety millions; and, in addition to this vast sum, there is an opening for an unlimited increase . . . . The indirect power of the bank cannot be stated in figures; but it can be shown to be immense. In the first place, it has the keeping of the public moneys, now amounting to twenty-six millions per annum . . . and the gratuitous use of the undrawn balances, large enough to constitute, in themselves, the capital of a great State bank. In the next place, its promissory notes are receivable, by law, in purchase of all property owned by the United States, and in payment of all debts due them. . . . In the third place, it wears the name of the United States, and has the federal government for a partner . . . . In the fourth place, it is armed with authority to . . . discredit the notes of other banks, by excluding them from all payments to the United States; and this, added to all its other powers, direct and indirect, makes this institution the uncontrollable monarch of the moneyed system of the Union. To whom is all this power granted? To a company of private individuals, many of them foreigners, and the mass of them residing in a remote and narrow corner of the Union, unconnected by any sympathy with the fertile regions of the Great Valley, in which the natural power of this Union—the power of numbers—will be found to reside long before the renewed term of a second charter would expire. By whom is all this power to be exercised? By a directory of seven (it may be), governed by a majority, of four (it may be); and none of these elected by the people, or responsible to them. Where is it to be exercised? At a single city, distant a thousand miles from some of the States, receiving the produce of none of them (except one); no interest in the welfare of any of them (except one); no commerce with the people; with branches in every State; and every branch subject to the secret and absolute orders of the supreme central head: thus constituting a system of centralism, hostile to the federative principle of our Union, encroaching upon the wealth and power of the States, and organized upon a principle to give the highest effect to the greatest power. . . .

Secondly. I object to the continuance of this bank, because its tendencies are dangerous and pernicious to the government and the people. . . .

It [the Bank] tends to aggravate the inequality of fortunes; to make the rich richer, and the poor poorer; to multiply nabobs and paupers; and to deepen and widen the gulf which separates Dives from Lazarus. A great moneyed power is favorable to great capitalists; for it is the principle of money to favor money. It is unfavorable to small capitalists; for it is the principle of money to eschew the needy and unfortunate. It is injurious to the laboring classes; because they receive no favors, and have the price of the property they wish to acquire raised to the paper maximum, while wages remain at the silver minimum.

IV

THE VETO

President Jackson did not disappoint his "anti-Bank" supporters. His veto message of July 10, 1832, is one of the most powerful and uncompromising statements of a President's political philosophy that has ever been uttered. □ James D. Richardson, Compiler, *Messages and Papers of the Presidents, 1789–1897,* Volume 2, pp. 576–579.

A bank of the United States is in many respects convenient for the Government and useful to the people. Entertaining this opinion, . . . [I am] impressed with the belief that some of the powers and privileges possessed by the existing bank are unauthorized by the Constitution, subversive of the rights of the States, and dangerous to the liberties of the people . . . .

It has been urged as an argument in favor of rechartering the present bank that the calling in its loans will produce great embarrassment and distress. The time allowed to close its concerns (four years) is ample, and if it has been well managed its pressure will be light, and heavy only in case its management has been bad. If, therefore, it shall produce distress, the fault will be its own, and it would furnish a reason against renewing a power which has been so obviously abused. But will there ever be a time when this reason will be less powerful? . . .

Is there no danger to our liberty and independence in a bank that in its nature has so little to bind it to our country? The president of the bank has told us that most of the State banks exist by its forbearance. Should its influence become concentered, as it may under the operation of such an act as this, in the hands of a self-elected directory whose interests are identified with those of the foreign stockholders, will there not be cause to tremble for the purity of our elections in peace and for the independence of our country in war? Their power would be great whenever they might choose to exert it; but if this monopoly were regularly renewed every fifteen or twenty years on terms proposed by themselves, they might seldom in peace put forth their strength to influence elections or control the affairs of the nation. But if any private citizen or public functionary should interpose to curtail its powers or prevent a renewal of its privileges, it can not be doubted that he would be made to feel its influence. . . .

It is to be regretted that the rich and powerful too often bend the acts of government to their selfish purposes. Distinctions in society will always exist under every just government. Equality of talents, of education, or of wealth can not be produced by human institutions. In the full enjoyment of the gifts of Heaven and the fruits of superior industry, economy, and virtue, every man is equally entitled to protection by law; but when the laws undertake to add to these natural and just advantages artificial distinctions, to grant titles, gratuities, and exclusive privileges, to make the rich richer and the potent more powerful, the humble members of society—the farmers, mechanics, and laborers—who have neither the time nor the means of securing like favors to themselves, have a right to complain of the injustice of their Government. There are no necessary evils in government. Its evils exist only in its abuses. If it would confine itself to equal protection, and, as Heaven does its rains, shower its favors alike on high and low, the rich and the poor, it would be an unqualified blessing. In the act before me there seems to be a wide and unnecessary departure from these just principles.

Nor is our Government to be maintained or our Union preserved by invasions of the rights and powers of the several States. In thus attempting to make our General Government strong we make it weak. Its true strength consists in leaving individuals and states as much as possible to themselves—in making itself felt, not in its power, but in its beneficence; not in its control, but in its protection; not in binding the States more closely to the center, but leaving each to move unobstructed in its proper orbit.

PROBLEM 2

The Boom

In 1830 the American economy was on a gradual upswing. By 1834, after a slight recession, the boom began. President Jackson had vetoed the act to recharter the second Bank of the United States, and a policy was adopted to place government deposits in certain private "pet" banks. Bankers thus no longer had to fear that the BUS would make embarrassing demands for specie. Financed by bank loans, business surged ahead. In eight industrial states the annual number of business incorporations doubled between 1830 and 1832 and they nearly doubled again by 1836. Between 1830 and 1836 exports rose almost 90 per cent and imports increased by 187 per cent. Tonnage hauled in the coasting trade and on inland waters shot up similarly.

A new network of railroads, turnpikes, and canals made the great expansion in domestic trade possible. Between 1820 and 1838 the states borrowed $60,000,000 for canals; $7,000,000 for roads; and $43,000,000 for railroads, largely from English investors. The construction of these internal improvements stimulated the economy, and the improvements themselves encouraged trade and mass production. The greatest boom, however, was in land speculation. The value of New York City real estate increased 150 per cent from 1830 to 1837, and in newer, western cities values increased several times that much. Promoters planted new towns across the prairies with less care than a farmer would give to planting a field of corn. Sales of land through federal government land offices in the Old Northwest (the area around the Great Lakes between Ohio and the Mississippi) rose from $2,100,000 in 1832 to $17,800,000 in 1836; in the Old Southwest (at that time, parts of Tennessee, Alabama, Mississippi, and Louisiana) they rose from $700,000 to $7,200,000.

Most of this increased economic activity was financed by credit from foreign loans and from the banks. Between 1830 and 1837 credit expanded two and a half times. Two thirds of this expansion could be attributed to the state-chartered private banks, which were growing steadily in number: in 1830, 330 banks had been chartered; in 1834, 506; and in 1837, 788. With the great profits to be made in loans, bank managers tended toward recklessness.

By 1835 many people were aware that a runaway boom was in progress and that it was bound to collapse. The question was when and how. But so long as money was plentiful and prices were high, most people enjoyed the prosperity without questioning its permanence. By all accounts it was an exciting time in which to live.

The selections in Problem 2 indicate the spirit of the times and the nature of the boom psychology. As you read, think about the following questions:

1 What facets of the American character most impressed foreigners? How would you judge the reliability of their accounts?

2 What characteristics of Americans, evident in these excerpts, might account for the speculative boom? Could Americans be energetic and hard-working as well as gamblers and speculators?

3 Did speculative practices in the East show any similarities to or differences from those in the Old Northwest? in the Old Southwest?

I

ECONOMIC ASPECTS OF AMERICAN CHARACTER

Alexis de Tocqueville, a brilliant young French historian and political scientist, visited the United States for nearly a year during 1831 and 1832. He recorded his impressions of America and Americans in his classic account *Democracy in America*. □ Alexis de Tocqueville, *Democracy in America*, Volume 2, pp. 167–168. New York: J. & H. G. Langley, copyright © 1841.

In the United States the greatest undertakings and speculations are executed without difficulty, because the whole population is engaged in productive industry, and because the poorest as well as the most opulent members of the commonwealth are ready to combine their efforts for these purposes. The consequence is, that a stranger is constantly amazed by the immense public works executed by a nation which contains, so to speak, no rich men. The Americans arrived but as yesterday on the territory which they inhabit, and they have already changed the whole order of nature for their own advantage. They have joined the Hudson to the Mississippi, and made the Atlantic Ocean communicate with the Gulf of Mexico, across a continent of more than five hundred leagues in extent which separates the two seas. The longest railroads which have been constructed up to the present time are in America.

But what most astonishes me in the United States, is not so much the marvellous grandeur of some undertakings, as the innumerable multitude of small ones. Almost all the farmers of the United States combine some trade with agriculture; most of them make agriculture itself a trade.

II

THE BUSINESS HABITS OF AMERICANS

Francis J. Grund, an Austrian of good family and education, settled in America about 1827. He became an ardent Jacksonian and a well-known journalist and educator. In the following excerpt he comments on some of the outstanding characteristics of his fellow citizens. □ Francis J. Grund, *The Americans*, p. 202. Boston: Marsh, Capen and Lyon, copyright © 1837.

There is probably no people on earth with whom business constitutes pleasure, and industry amusement, in an equal degree with the inhabitants of the United States of America. Active occupation is not only the principal source of their happiness, and the foundation of their natural greatness, but they are absolutely wretched without it, and instead of the "*dolce far niente* [pleasantly doing nothing]," know but the horrors of idleness. Business is the very soul of an American; he pursues it, not as a means of procuring for himself and his family the necessary comforts of life, but as the fountain of all human felicity; and shows as much enthusiastic ardour in his application to it as any crusader ever evinced for the conquest of the Holy Land, or the followers of Mohammed for the spreading of the Koran.

From the earliest hour in the morning till late at night the streets, offices, and warehouses of the large cities are thronged by men of all trades and professions, each following his vocation like a *perpetuum mobile* [continually moving thing], as if he never dreamt of cessation from labour, or the possibility of becoming fatigued.

III

NEWSPAPER COMMENT ON SPECULATION IN THE 1830'S

On May 9, 1835, the *Niles Weekly Register,* a popular newspaper published in Baltimore, collected stories from other journals about the speculative mania that had spread through the country. ☐ "Speculation! Speculation!! Speculation!!!" Baltimore: *Niles Weekly Register,* Volume 48, Number 1233, May 9, 1835, pp. 167–168.

We shall offer a selection of articles as to what is going on, in the way of "speculation." Verily, the people are mad!

FROM THE NATIONAL GAZETTE.

. . . [Speculation] in stocks and real property is more general and extravagant than it has been before . . . , in all our principal cities. A gambling spirit is apt to prove epidemic, and becomes violent in proportion to its spread. It seizes on men in all sorts of circumstances, diverting them from the regular pursuits and hopes of industry, and stimulating them to risks by which their minds are kept in extreme agitation, and all their means exposed to sudden and ruinous vicissitudes. We are told by intelligent gentlemen who have been lookers on, of late, at Boston, New York and in our own city, that multitudes are now prominent and desperate dealers in the stock and other speculation markets, of classes and ages, callings and positions in life, that formerly were never seen nor expected, and themselves never thought of acting, in such scenes. Small tradesmen, shopkeepers, clerks of all degrees, operatives of town and country, members of the learned professions, students in the offices, beginners in the world without capital, or with a little, all frequent the exchanges and the auction-grounds to try their fortunes as with the lotteries. They chase bubbles not less intently than those who have leisure and money to spare. We scarcely need add that this diffusive excitement, subject as it is to rumors and various chances of the day or hour, is unfavorable to productive industry, to steady habits and sure aims, and to morals, which are always more or less in danger when hazard whets cupidity, governs action, and determines fate in a general whirl of spirits and thoughts.

FROM THE PHILADELPHIA GAZETTE.

Pennsylvania and Ohio canal. The improvement is one of the most important to Philadelphia, that has ever been projected. The books for subscription to the capital stock, were opened this morning at 10 o'clock, at the exchange, and the competition for access to the room was of the most lively kind. The whole number of shares offered, being 6,000 in number, were taken in less than half an hour. . . .

FROM THE NEW YORK EVENING STAR.

Yesterday, after the extravagant rise of stock, and the immense sales had taken place at the board, it was suggested that their room was not half large enough to accommodate their numbers, and that a larger place must be procured. One of the gentlemen said he understood there were excellent accommodations that could be had at the *"Lunatic Asylum."*

IV

SPECULATION IN THE WEST

Land "development" extended from the Atlantic Ocean westward, and speculation became wilder and wilder as one traveled west. The following account by William Leggett, an assistant editor of the New York *Evening Post*, appeared on September 14, 1836. □ Theodore Sedgwick, Jr., Editor, *A Collection of the Political Writings of William Leggett*, Volume 2, pp. 83–85. New York: Taylor and Dodd, copyright © 1840.

A traveller, once, in Indiana, on setting out early one morning from the place where he had passed the night, consulted his map of the country, and finding that a very considerable town called . . . Vienna . . . occupied a point on his road but some twelve or fifteen miles off, concluded to journey as far as that place before breakfast. Another equally extensive town . . . was laid down at a convenient distance for his afternoon stage; and there he proposed halting for the night. He continued to travel at a good round pace until the sun had attained a great height in heaven, and until he computed that he had accomplished more than twice or thrice the distance which he proposed to himself in the outset. . . . Still he saw no town before him, even of the humblest kind, much less such a magnificent one as his map had prepared him to look for. At length, meeting a solitary wood-chopper emerging from the forest, he accosted him, and inquired how far it was to Vienna. "Vienna!" exclaimed the man, "why you passed it five and twenty miles back: did you not notice a stick of hewn timber and a blazed tree beside the road? That was Vienna." The dismayed traveller then inquired how far it was to the other place, at which he designed passing the night. "Why you are right on that place now," returned the man; "it begins just the other side of yon ravine, and runs down to a clump of girdled trees which you will see about a mile further on the road." "And are there no houses built?" faltered out the traveller, who began to suspect that, as the song says—"The heath this night must be his bed."

"Oh, no houses whatsomever," returned the woodman; "they hewed and hauled the logs for a blacksmith's shop, but before they raised it the town lots were all disposed of in the eastern states, and every thing has been left just as you now see it ever since."

It is pretty much in the same way that things are left, at the present time, in this portion of the country. If any one should make a map of the lands lying within the compass of some thirty or forty miles from this city, and embrace in it all the improvements, projected as well as actually existing, the spectator, who does not know the true condition of the country, would be astonished at the appearance of dense population which it would present. Cities, towns and villages would be represented as lying scattered around him at every step. The intermediate slips of unoccupied ground would seem hardly large enough even to furnish pasture for the stray cattle of the surrounding towns, much less to supply their inhabitants with all the necessary products of agricultural consumption. We hear no more, now-a-days, of a farm being sold, as a farm, in the vicinity of the city. The land is all divided into lots of a hundred feet by twenty-five; and it would seem as if, in the visions of speculators, a dense city must soon extend from the Atlantic ocean to the lakes, and from the Hudson river to the borders of Connecticut.

V

CHICAGO, THAT WONDERFUL TOWN

Harriet Martineau, a prominent English author, arrived in Chicago during the great land sales in 1836 when the town was crowded with speculators hoping to make fortunes. Miss Martineau described Chicago as she saw it. □ Harriet Martineau, *Society in America,* Volume 1, pp. 259–261. New York: Saunders and Otley, copyright © 1837.

I never saw a busier place than Chicago was at the time of our arrival. The streets were crowded with land speculators, hurrying from one sale to another. A Negro, dressed up in scarlet, bearing a scarlet flag, and riding a white horse with housings of scarlet, announced the times of sale. At every street-corner where he stopped, the crowd flocked around him; and it seemed as if some prevalent mania infected the whole people. The rage for speculation might fairly be so regarded. As the gentlemen of our party walked the streets, store-keepers hailed them from their doors, with offers of farms, and all manner of land-lots, advising them to speculate before the price of land rose higher. A young lawyer, of my acquaintance there, had realized five hundred dollars per day, the five preceding days, by merely making out titles to land. Another friend had realized, in two years, ten times as much money as he had before fixed upon as a competence for life. Of course, this rapid money-making is a merely temporary evil. A bursting of the bubble must come soon. The absurdity of the speculation is so striking, that the wonder is that the fever should have attained such a height as I witnessed. The immediate occasion of the bustle which prevailed, the week we were at Chicago, was the sale of lots, to the value of two millions of dollars, along the course of a projected canal; and of another set, immediately behind these. . . . Whereas, wild land on the banks of a canal, not yet even marked out, was selling at Chicago for more than rich land, well improved, in the finest part of the valley of the Mohawk, on the banks of a canal which is already the medium of an almost inestimable amount of traffic. If sharpers and gamblers were to be the sufferers by the impending crash at Chicago, no one would feel much concerned; but they, unfortunately, are the people who encourage the delusion, in order to profit by it. Many a high-spirited, but inexperienced, young man; many a simple settler, will be ruined for the advantage of knaves.

VI

BOOM IN THE OLD SOUTHWEST

The lure of cotton riches drew Southern planters, immigrants, adventurers, and scoundrels to parts of Tennessee, Alabama, Mississippi, and Louisiana. The following selection is from a description of that Old Southwest region in the flush times of the 1830's. Joseph Baldwin, the author, was a self-taught lawyer who emigrated to Mississippi from Virginia to avoid competition with the formally educated barristers of the East. □ Joseph Baldwin, *The Flush Times of Alabama and Mississippi,* pp. 82–87. New York: D. Appleton and Company, copyright © 1853.

This country was just settling up. Marvellous accounts had gone forth of the fertility of its virgin lands; and the productions of the soil were commanding a price remunerating to slave labor as it had never been remunerated before. Emigrants came flocking in from all quarters of the Union, especially from the slaveholding States. The new country seemed to be a reservoir, and every road leading to it a vagrant stream of enterprise and adventure. Money, or what passed for money, was the only cheap thing to be had. Every cross-road and every avocation presented an opening, —through which a fortune was seen by the adventurer in near perspective. Credit was a thing of course. To refuse it—if the thing was ever done— were an insult for which a bowie knife were not a too summary or exemplary a means of redress. The State banks were issuing their bills by the sheet . . . ; and no other showing was asked of the applicant for the loan than an authentication of his great distress for money. Finance, even in its most exclusive quarter, had thus already got, in this wonderful revolution, to work upon the principles of the charity hospital. If an overseer grew tired of supervising a plantation and felt a call to the mercantile life, even if he omitted the compendious method of buying out a merchant wholesale, stock, house and good will, and laying down, at once, his bullwhip for the yard-stick—all he had to do was to go on to New-York, and present himself in Pearl-street with a letter avouching his citizenship, and a clean shirt, and he was regularly given a through ticket to speedy bankruptcy.

Under this stimulating process prices rose like smoke. Lots in obscure villages were held at city prices; lands, bought at the minimum cost of government, were sold at from thirty to forty dollars per acre, and considered dirt cheap at that. In short, the country had got to be a full antetype of California, in all except the gold. . . .

"Commerce was king"—and Rags, Tag and Bobtail his cabinet council. Rags was treasurer. Banks, chartered on a specie basis, did a very flourishing business on the promissory notes of the individual stockholders ingeniously substituted in lieu of cash. They issued ten for one, the *one* being fictitious. They generously loaned all the directors could not use themselves, and were not choice whether Bardolph was the endorser for Falstaff, or Falstaff borrowed on his own proper credit, or the funds advanced him by Shallow. The stampede towards the golden temple became general: the delusion prevailed far and wide that this thing was not a burlesque on commerce and finance. Even the directors of the banks began to have their doubts whether the intended swindle was not a failure. Like Lord Clive, when reproached for extortion to the extent of some millions in Bengal, they exclaimed, after the bubble burst, "When they thought of what they had got, and what they might have got, they were astounded at their own moderation."

PROBLEM 3

The Panic

By 1836 when enormous public land sales had piled up a treasury surplus of $37,500,000, Congress thought it might be politically advantageous to distribute this surplus among the states. The Distribution Act was passed in June, authorizing the eighty-eight private "pet" banks, which received government deposits, to carry out the distribution of funds. These banks were to pay the funds to the states in specie, or in notes fully backed by specie, and to make the first payment on January 1, 1837. To accumulate enough specie, banks were forced to contract credit and to reduce the number of bank notes in circulation.

This predicament among the banks was intensified by the famous Specie Circular of July 11, 1836, issued by order of President Andrew Jackson. In an attempt to decrease land speculation, the President specified that all payments for public lands must be made in specie after August 15, 1836. Men who had expected to make payments for their real estate purchases in bank notes had to find specie with which to pay or default and thus lose their lands.

These two measures—the Distribution Act of June 1836 and the Specie Circular—touched off a wild scramble for specie. As the amount of available specie steadily decreased, people began to hoard gold and silver money. The dearth of specie that resulted and the consequent contraction of bank notes in circulation (because of diminished specie reserves in bank vaults) forced banks to reduce their loans.

Nevertheless, economic activity remained high during the remainder of 1836. In the fall of the year, however, the specie shortage in America began to affect the economy of Great Britain. Americans had been importing large quantities of gold from Britain (through such means as sales of farm products and shares in business ventures) to meet the specie shortage. To stop the outward flow of metal, the Bank of England raised interest rates and refused to pay American suppliers of commodities in specie. This policy created a crisis in New York banks, for their supplies of gold were thus diminished at the same time that banks west of New York were draining them of specie.

Then between August 1836 and June 1837 the price of cotton fell by nearly 50 per cent. Cotton was the most important source of foreign earnings for the United States. With this reduction in price, planters found themselves unable to repay loans. Southern banks began to fail, affecting the eastern banks with which they were associated. By May 10 all New York banks were refusing to exchange specie for paper. English banks followed suit.

In the wake of these events, British commodity exports to the United States fell 60 per cent and the export of British capital to the United States diminished drastically.

The collapse of the financial structure produced a panic. Business firms failed by the hundreds, and workers were turned away from factory doors. In the West and South thousands of farmers lost their lands. Paper fortunes were wiped out overnight.

The fall and winter of 1837 gave the American people ample time to contemplate the results of their hectic pursuit of wealth.

The readings in Problem 3 examine the causes of the panic and describe its dimensions.

As you read, think about the following questions:

1   On what grounds did Jackson defend his policies? Were economic considerations paramount in his decisions?

2   What was the crux of the disagreement between Biddle and Leggett? Which of these two men had the better argument about the cause of the financial distress in 1837?

3   What role did actions by President Jackson play in the Panic of 1837?

I

THE SPECIE CIRCULAR

Seldom has a presidential announcement as brief as the Specie Circular caused such an impact on the economy. Its precise effects and the wisdom of the act have been a subject of controversy from the day it was issued, July 11, 1836. ☐ Asbury Dickens, *American State Papers, Public Lands,* Volume 8, p. 910. Washington, D.C.: United States Congress.

The President of the United States has given directions, and you are hereby instructed, after the 15th day of August next, to receive in payment of the public lands nothing except what is directed by the existing laws, viz.: gold and silver. . . .

The principal objects of the President, in adopting this measure, being to repress alleged frauds, and to withhold any countenance or facilities in the power of the government from the monopoly of the public lands in the hands of speculators and capitalists, to the injury of the actual settlers in the new States, and of emigrants in search of new homes, as well as to discourage the ruinous extension of bank issues and bank credits, by which those results are generally supposed to be promoted, your utmost vigilance is required, and relied on, to carry this order into complete execution.

II

JACKSONIAN ECONOMICS

So that his action could not be countermanded, President Jackson waited to issue the Specie Circular until after Congress had adjourned. Among Congressmen who approved Jackson's decision, Senator Thomas Hart Benton of Missouri noted that the President issued the Circular "in known disregard of the will both of the majority of Congress and of his cabinet." Against those who disapproved of the order, Jackson boldly defended his action in his last annual message in December 1836. ☐ James D. Richardson, Compiler, *Messages and Papers of the Presidents, 1789–1897,* Volume 3, pp. 249–250. Washington, D.C.: Authority of Congress. Copyright © 1897 by James D. Richardson.

The effects of an extension of bank credits and overissues of bank paper have been strikingly illustrated in the sales of the public lands. From the returns made by the various registers and receivers in the early part of last summer it was perceived that the receipts arising from the sales of the public lands were increasing to an unprecedented amount. In effect, however, these receipts amounted to nothing more than credits in bank. The banks lent out their notes to speculators. They were paid to the receivers and imme- diately·returned to the banks, to be lent out again and again, being mere instruments to transfer to speculators the most valuable public land and pay the Government by a credit on the books of the banks. . . . The spirit of expansion and speculation was not confined to the deposit banks, but per- vaded the whole multitude of banks throughout the Union and was giving rise to new institutions to aggravate the evil.

The safety of the public funds and the interest of the people generally required that these operations should be checked; and it became the duty of every branch of the General and State Governments to adopt all legitimate and proper means to produce that salutary effect. Under this view of my duty I directed the issuing of the order which will be laid before you by the Secretary of the Treasury, requiring payment for the public lands sold to be made in specie, with an exception until the 15th of the present month in favor of actual settlers. This measure has produced many salutary conse- quences. It checked the career of the Western banks and gave them additional strength in anticipation of the pressure which has since pervaded our Eastern as well as the European commercial cities. By preventing the extension of the credit system it measurably cut off the means of speculation and retarded its progress in monopolizing the most valuable of the public lands. It has tended to save the new States from a nonresident proprietorship, one of the greatest obstacles to the advancement of a new country and the prosperity of an old one. It has tended to keep open the public lands for entry [purchase] by emigrants at Government prices instead of their being com- pelled to purchase of speculators at double or triple prices. And it is conveying into the interior large sums in silver and gold, there to enter permanently into the currency of the country and place it on a firmer foundation.

III

"OLD HICKORY" DEFENDS HIS FINANCIAL POLICIES

Land speculation had been the mainstay of the boom. Once it was halted, trouble was sure to follow. By the time Jackson left office the country was on the brink of financial collapse. Jackson's policies were being assailed on all sides, but in his farewell address "Old Hickory" fought back, warning his fellow citizens that paper money, speculation, and concentrated economic power would destroy their liberty. ☐ James D. Richardson, Compiler, *Messages and Papers of the Presidents, 1789–1897*, Volume 3, pp. 301–302, 306.

In reviewing the conflicts which have taken place between different interests in the United States and the policy pursued since the adoption of our present form of Government, we find nothing that has produced such deep-seated evil as the course of legislation in relation to the currency. The Constitution of the United States unquestionably intended to secure to the people a circulating medium of gold and silver. But the establishment of a national bank by Congress, with the privilege of issuing paper money receivable in the payment of the public dues, and the unfortunate course of legislation in the several States upon the same subject, drove from general circulation the constitutional currency and substituted one of paper in its place. . . .

The paper system being founded on public confidence and having of itself no intrinsic value, it is liable to great and sudden fluctuations, thereby rendering property insecure and the wages of labor unsteady and uncertain. The corporations which create the paper money can not be relied upon to keep the circulating medium uniform in amount. In times of prosperity, when confidence is high, they are tempted by the prospect of gain or by the influence of those who hope to profit by it to extend their issues of paper beyond the bounds of discretion and the reasonable demands of business; and when these issues have been pushed on from day to day, until public confidence is at length shaken, then a reaction takes place, and they immediately withdraw the credits they have given, suddenly curtail their issues, and produce an unexpected and ruinous contraction of the circulating medium, which is felt by the whole community. The banks by this means save themselves, and the mischievous consequences of their imprudence or cupidity are visited upon the public. Nor does the evil stop here. These ebbs and flows in the currency and these indiscreet extensions of credit naturally engender a spirit of speculation injurious to the habits and character of the people. We have already seen its effects in the wild spirit of speculation in the public lands and various kinds of stock which within the last year or two seized upon such a multitude of our citizens and threatened to pervade all classes of society and to withdraw their attention from the sober pursuits of honest industry. It is not by encouraging this spirit that we shall best preserve public virtue and promote the true interests of our country; but if your currency continues as exclusively paper as it now is, it will foster this eager desire to amass wealth without labor; it will multiply the number of dependents on bank accommodations and bank favors; the temptation to obtain money at any sacrifice will become stronger and stronger, and inevitably lead to corruption, which will find its way into your public councils and destroy at no distant day the purity of your Government.

IV

NICHOLAS BIDDLE ON THE CAUSE OF THE PANIC

When the financial structure collapsed in 1837, Nicholas Biddle was not in doubt as to its cause. In a letter to John Quincy Adams, he laid the responsibility squarely upon Jackson's policies. □ Nicholas Biddle, *Two Letters to the Hon. J. Quincy Adams; Embracing a history of the re-charter of the Bank of the United States; and a view of the present condition of the currency*, pp. 16–18. London: P. Richardson, copyright © 1837.

On a sudden, without any intimation of the coming shock, an order was issued by the Secretary, declaring that [bank] . . . notes were no longer receivable, and of course inviting all who held the notes, and had deposits in these banks, to convert them into specie. . . .

The commercial community were thus taken by surprise. The interior banks making no loans, and converting their Atlantic funds into specie, the debtors in the interior could make no remittances to the merchants in the Atlantic cities, who are thus thrown for support on the banks of those cities at a moment when they are unable to afford relief . . . .

By this unnatural process the specie of New York and the other commercial cities is piled up in the western states, not circulated, not used, but held as a defense against the Treasury—and while the West cannot use it—the East is suffering for the want of it. The result is, that the commercial intercourse between the West and the Atlantic is almost wholly suspended . . . . In November, 1836, the interest of money has risen to 24 per cent—merchants are struggling to preserve their credit by ruinous sacrifices—and it costs five or six times as much to transmit funds from the west and southwest, as it did in November, 1835. . . . Thus while the exchanges with all the world are in our favor—while Europe is alarmed, and the Bank of England itself uneasy at the quantity of specie we possess—we are suffering, because, from mere mismanagement, the whole ballast of the currency is shifted from one side of the vessel to the other.

Then as to the banks. It is quite probable that many of the banks have extended their issues—but whose fault is it? Who called these banks into existence? The Executive. Who tempted and goaded them to these issues? Undoubtedly the Executive. The country five years ago was in possession of the most beautiful machinery of currency and exchanges the world ever saw. It consisted of a number of state banks protected, and, at the same time, restrained by the Bank of the United States.

The people of the United States through their representatives rechartered that institution. But the Executive, discontented with its independence, rejected the act of Congress—and the favorite topic of declamation was that the states would make banks, and that these banks could create a better system of currency and exchanges. The states accordingly made banks—and then followed idle parades about the loans of these banks, and their enlarged dealings in exchange. And what is the consequence? The Bank of the United States has not ceased to exist more than seven months, and already the whole currency and exchanges are running into inextricable confusion, and the industry of the country is burthened with extravagant charges on all the commercial intercourse of the Union. And now, when these banks have been created by the Executive, and urged into these excesses, instead of gentle and gradual remedies, a fierce crusade is raised against them—the funds are harshly and suddenly taken from them, and they are forced to extraordinary means of defense against the very power which brought them into being. They received, and were expected to receive, in payment for the Government, the notes of each other, and the notes of other banks, and the facility with which they did so, was a ground of special commendation by the Government. And now that Government has let loose upon them a demand for specie, to the whole amount of these notes.

V

"THE CAUSE LIES DEEPER"

Although the majority of informed Americans supported Biddle's view of financial affairs, a few influential men rallied to Jackson's cause. Among them was William Leggett. □ Theodore Sedgwick, Jr., Editor, *A Collection of the Political Writings of William Leggett,* Volume 2, pp. 102–105. New York: Taylor and Dodd, copyright © 1840.

But the first, great, and all important cause of the pecuniary distress lies much deeper than any which the opposition papers assign. It is neither the Treasury order in relation to the public lands, nor the Treasury orders on . . .

[deposit] banks. These last have, at the very worst, but precipitated an evil, which, had no such orders been issued, or no transfers in any way made, could by no possibility have been long averted. . . .

Without the distribution bill, even, a dreadful commercial revulsion could not long have been avoided. We were rushing on madly at a rate which could not long be continued. . . . Look at the present state of the country. When did it ever before present such a spectacle of prodigiously distended credit? When did such a fever of speculation madden the brains of whole communities? When did all sorts of commodities bear such enormous prices? And when, at the same time, was there ever such vast consumption—such prodigality, wastefulness, and unthinking profusion? Is the treasury order the cause of this? Alas, it is one of its remote consequences. What filled your treasury to such overflowing, that some cunning politician was prompted by a consideration of the exuberance to devise the scheme of distribution? Speculation. What excited that spirit of speculation? The sudden and enormous increase of bank capital, and the corresponding inflation of bank currency. In the last eighteen months alone *nearly one hundred millions of bank capital* have been added to the previous amount.

. . . The business of the country has been stimulated into most unwholesome and fatal activity. Circumstances, unlooked for, have occurred to aggravate the epidemic frenzy. The government has obtained the payment of long delayed indemnities from foreign powers; and new formed corporations have contracted large loans abroad. These sums, added to the product of our staples, have been exhausted by the excessive importations. Domestic speculation—speculation in the products of home consumption, in land, in town lots, in houses, in stock enterprises, in every thing, has kept pace, step for step, with the inordinate increase of foreign trade. What is to pay all this vast accumulation of debt? It must come at last out of labour. It must come from the products of industry. We have been borrowing largely of the future, and have at last arrived at the point where we must pause, and wait for the farmer, the mechanic, and patient hewer of wood and drawer of water to relieve us from our difficulties.

VI

"THE SPLENDID LIE"

Arguments on what caused the panic did little to console those who suffered from its effects. The Southwest, which then included parts of Tennessee, Alabama, Mississippi, and Louisiana, had seen the greatest excesses in speculation and was hit harder than any other section of the country. Joseph Baldwin, who had become a successful lawyer in Alabama and Mississippi by 1836, published a series of sketches about life in that region, from which the following selection is taken. ☐ Joseph G. Baldwin, *The Flush Times of Alabama and Mississippi,* pp. 90–91. New York: D. Appleton and Company, copyright © 1853.

. . . [The] Specie Circular was issued without warning, and the splendid lie of a false credit burst into fragments. . . . Gen. Jackson . . . did some very pretty . . . work, in converting the bank bills back again into rags and oak-leaves. Men worth a million were insolvent for two millions: promising young cities marched back again into the wilderness. The ambitious town plat was re-annexed to the plantation, like a country girl taken home from the city. The frolic was ended, and what headaches, and feverish limbs the next morning! . . . Where are ye now my ruffing gallants? Where now the braw cloths and watch chains and rings and fine horses? Alas! for ye—they are glimmering among the things that were—the wonder of an hour! They live only in memory, as unsubstantial as the promissory notes ye gave for them. When it came to be tested, the whole matter was found to be hollow and fallacious. . . .

Such is a charcoal sketch of the interesting region—now inferior to none in resources, and the character of its population—during the FLUSH TIMES; a period constituting an episode in the commercial history of the world—the reign of humbug, and wholesale insanity, just overthrown in time to save the whole country from ruin. But while it lasted, many of our countrymen came into the South-West in time to get "a benefit."

PROBLEM 4

The Early 1840's

Problems 1 through 3 have traced the banking history of the United States and examined the social setting in which economic events took place. They have not, however, indicated whether or not the financial collapse alone was responsible for the depression which struck the country in the years which followed. This issue—the cause of the depression—has long interested economic historians; they have debated the issue for years in books and journals, but there has been little agreement.

The depression of the early 1840's had effects in both Europe and America. When American companies and many of the states defaulted on, that is, failed to pay, their debts, foreign creditors were incensed. Many Englishmen refused to invest further money in America because they feared to lose it. Stopping this cross-Atlantic flow of funds restricted the pace at which the American economy could grow.

The effects of the depression within the United States were far more noticeable. Merchants and traders, especially those involved in trade with Great Britain, suffered heavy losses as the volume of business declined. Market farmers, especially men whose main product was cotton, found their incomes sharply reduced. Business incorporations dwindled. City workers, whose jobs were affected by the drop in marketing and manufacturing, were put out of work by the failure of factories and stores. All Americans felt the economic decline in some degree. Only those persons who tilled small farms and were not dependent on marketing their products escaped the brunt of the hard times. They were least affected by the falling price of cotton and the inability to borrow money from a bank.

Problem 4 contributes two types of evidence to the Unit. The first consists of tables of statistics about a number of economic matters. The other excerpts in the Problem examine the effects of the depression in England and in various parts of the United States. As you read, keep the following questions in mind:

1   According to the figures in the tables, when did the worst of the depression strike? Which sections of the country appeared to suffer most?

2   What factor might have been crucial in affecting the personal attitudes of Lyell and Smith?

3   In what respects is Brownson's attack on private banks like or unlike Senator Benton's criticism of the second Bank of the United States in his speech in Problem 1?

4   Would you say the selection by Brownson is mainly concerned with studying causes of the depression? Do you think bad times primarily shaped Brownson's thinking?

I

SOME STATISTICAL INDICATORS

The regions of the United States and its territories in the early nineteenth century were roughly designated as the Northeast, the South (Old South, New South, and the Old Southwest), and the West. Ohio was included in the West. The degree of western expansion and the value of western crops was reflected in the number of incorporations, or formation of new business enterprises, that occurred in the West. During periods of rising cotton prices, planters were encouraged to buy land in the New South (Florida, Alabama, Mississippi, Louisiana, and Arkansas) and to set up new plantations. Sales of virgin land preceded production from those lands by three to four years.

Between 1836 and 1840 the United States exported commodities, such as cotton, tobacco, rice, wheat, flour, manufactured goods, and lumber, with cotton constituting more than 50 per cent of the total export values. Imports consisted mainly of manufactured goods from Britain and France and of coffee, tea, sugar, and cocoa from Cuba and the West Indies. After the Panic of 1837, the succeeding depression years found many American state governments and private corporations defaulting on debts to foreign investors.

The following tables provide some indication of when the worst of the depression struck and which parts of the nation were hit hardest. ☐ All tables reprinted from Douglass C. North, *The Economic Growth of the United States, 1790–1860*, pp. 232, 233, 234, 238, 256, 261. Englewood Cliffs, New Jersey: Prentice-Hall, Inc., copyright © 1961.

Table 1 by permission of the National Bureau of Economic Research, Inc. George H. Evans, Jr., *Business Incorporations in the United States, 1800–1943*, p. 18. New York: National Bureau of Economic Research, Inc., copyright © 1948.

Tables 2 and 3 by permission of Harvard University Press. Arthur H. Cole, "Cyclical and Sectional Variations in the Sale of Public Lands, 1816–1860." Cambridge, Massachusetts: *The Review of Economics and Statistics*, Volume 9, Number 1, January 1927, p. 52.

Tables 4, 5, 6, 7, and 8 by permission of Prentice-Hall, Inc.

TABLES 1 AND 2

Do these tables indicate any relationship between land sales in the seven western states and business conditions in Ohio? What kind of corporations were those in Ohio most likely to be?

1			2		
ANNUAL INCORPORATIONS			PUBLIC LAND SALES		
OHIO			WESTERN STATES[1]		
			in thousands of dollars		
Year	Number		Year	Receipts	
1834	31		1834	2,807	
1835	38		1835	9,007	
1836	71		1836	17,765	
1837	92		1837	5,374	
1838	55		1838	3,195	
1839	67		1839	5,192	
1840	10		1840	2,251	
1841	9		1841	1,212	
1842	11		1842	1,137	
1843	10		1843	1,568	
1844	29		1844	1,872	
1845	53		1845	2,163	

[1] Illinois, Indiana, Iowa, Michigan, Missouri, Ohio, Wisconsin.

TABLES 3, 4, AND 5

The tables in this group enable the student to make an analysis of certain fundamental changes which occurred in the cotton-growing industry between the years 1834 and 1845. How are these three statistical tables related?

What could you infer about the profitability of growing cotton in each of the years shown in Tables 3, 4, and 5?

3		4		5	
PUBLIC LAND SALES SOUTHERN STATES[1] in thousands of dollars		COTTON PRICES in cents, per pound		VALUE OF COTTON EXPORTS	
Year	Receipts	Year	Price	Year	Price
1834	3,256	1834	12.90	1834	49,448,402
1835	7,159	1835	17.45	1835	64,961,302
1836	7,170	1836	16.50	1836	71,284,925
1837	1,568	1837	13.25	1837	63,240,102
1838	817	1838	10.14	1838	61,556,811
1839	1,297	1839	13.36	1839	61,238,982
1840	497	1840	8.92	1840	63,870,307
1841	299	1841	9.50	1841	54,330,341
1842	315	1842	7.85	1842	47,593,464
1843	481	1843	7.25	1843	49,119,806
1844	368	1844	7.73	1844	54,063,501
1845	299	1845	5.63	1845	51,739,643

[1]Alabama, Arkansas, Florida, Louisiana, Mississippi.

TABLES 6, 7, AND 8

These tables indicate that our foreign indebtedness declined as our trade declined. Why? What was the relationship between United States foreign indebtedness and the prosperity of the country during these years?

6		7		8	
VALUE OF EXPORTS in dollars		VALUE OF IMPORTS in dollars		FOREIGN INDEBTEDNESS in millions of dollars	
Year	Total Exports	Year	Total Imports	Year	Indebtedness
1834	102,260,000	1834	110,782,000	1834	128.0
1835	115,216,000	1835	139,499,000	1835	158.1
1836	124,339,000	1836	180,111,000	1836	220.3
1837	111,443,000	1837	133,082,000	1837	242.9
1838	104,979,000	1838	97,889,000	1838	248.1
1839	112,252,000	1839	159,627,000	1839	297.2
1840	123,669,000	1840	100,224,000	1840	266.4
1841	111,817,000	1841	125,417,000	1841	262.0
1842	99,878,000	1842	97,997,000	1842	243.8
1843	82,826,000	1843	43,282,000	1843	221.6
1844	105,746,000	1844	104,657,000	1844	216.8
1845	106,040,000	1845	115,448,000	1845	213.0

II

THE DEPRESSION AT THE LOCAL LEVEL

An English traveler, Sir Charles Lyell, visited Philadelphia in 1842 and described how the depression affected American men, women, and children. He indicated the international ramifications of the economic collapse.   □ Sir Charles Lyell, *Travels in North America*, Volume 1, pp. 173–174. New York: Wiley and Putnam, copyright © 1845.

It was painful to witness the ruin and distress occasioned by this last blow, following, as it did, so many previous disasters. Men advanced in years, and retired from active life, after success in business, or at the bar, or after military service, too old to migrate with their families to the West, and begin the world again, are left destitute; many widows and single women have lost their all, and great numbers of the poorer classes are deprived of their savings. An erroneous notion prevails in England that the misery created by these bankruptcies is confined chiefly to foreigners, but, in fact, many of the poorest citizens of Pennsylvania, and of other States, had invested money in these securities. . . .

The debt of Pennsylvania amounted to about 8,000,000*l.* sterling, nearly two thirds of which was held by British owners; and as a majority of these belonged to that party which always indulged the most sanguine hopes of the prospects of the American republic, and estimated most highly the private worth of the people and their capacity for self-government, they suffered doubly, being disappointed alike in their pecuniary speculations and their political views. It was natural, therefore, that a re-action of feeling should embitter their minds, and incline them to magnify and exaggerate the iniquity of that conduct which had at once impugned the soundness of their judgment, and inflicted a severe injury on their fortunes. Hence, not a few of them, confounding together the different States, have represented all the Americans as little better than swindlers, who, having defrauded Europe of many millions sterling, were enjoying tranquilly and with impunity the fruits of their knavery. The public works executed with foreign capital are supposed by many in England to yield a large profit on the outlay, which is not the case in any one of the delinquent States.

The loss or temporary suspension of the interest even of one third of the above-mentioned debt, in a country like Pennsylvania, where there is a small amount of capital to invest, and that belonging chiefly to persons incapable of exerting themselves to make money, a country where property is so much divided, and where such extensive failures had preceded this crisis, inflicts a far deeper wound on the happiness of the community, than the defalcation of a much larger sum in Great Britain would occasion.

III

A VIEW FROM LONDON

The Englishman in London who saw American affairs only through the pages of newspapers viewed the financial troubles in America differently from Sir Charles Lyell. Sydney Smith, a London wit who lost heavily when Pennsylvania could not pay its debts, wrote the following letter to the *London Morning Chronicle* in November 1843. ☐ Sydney Smith, *Works*, Volume 3, pp. 446–448. London: Longman, Brown, Green, and Longmans, copyright © 1848.

I never meet a Pennsylvanian at a London dinner without feeling a disposition to seize and divide him;—to allot his beaver [hat] to one sufferer and his coat to another— . . . his pocket-handkerchief to the orphan, and to comfort the widow with his silver watch, Broadway rings, and the London Guide, which he always carries in his pockets. How such a man can set himself down at an English table without feeling that he owes two or three pounds to every man in company I am at a loss to conceive: he has no more right to eat with honest men than a leper has to eat with clean men. If he has a particle of honour in his composition he should shut himself up, and say, "I cannot mingle with you, I belong to a degraded people—I must hide myself—I am a plunderer from Pennsylvania."

Figure to yourself a Pennsylvanian receiving foreigners in his own country, walking over the public works with them, and showing them Larcenous Lake, Swindling Swamp, Crafty Canal, and Rogues' Railway, and other dishonest works. "This swamp we gained (says the patriotic borrower) by the repudiated loan of 1828. Our canal robbery was in 1830; we pocketed your good people's money for the railroad only last year." All this may seem very smart to the Americans; but if I had the misfortune to be born among such a people, the land of my fathers should not retain me a single moment after the act of repudiation. I would appeal from my fathers to my forefathers. I would fly to Newgate [prison] for greater purity of thought . . . .

. . . I have a general feeling, that by that breed of men I have been robbed and ruined, and I shudder and keep aloof. The pecuniary credit of every State is affected by Pennsylvania. Ohio pays; but with such a bold bankruptcy before their eyes how long will Ohio pay? The truth is, that the eyes of all capitalists are averted from the United States. The finest commercial under-standings will have nothing to do with them. Men rigidly just, who penetrate boldly into the dealings of nations, and work with vigour and virtue for honourable wealth—great and high-minded merchants—will loathe, and are now loathing, the name of America: it is becoming, since its fall, the common-sewer of Europe, and the native home of the needy villain.

IV

EXODUS IN THE 1840'S

Many cotton planters, ruined by the depression, could not fulfill their obli-gations, and they fled their plantations to escape creditors. Jehu A. Orr, a young lawyer engaged in the pursuit of some of these planters, described the effects of the depression which he saw.   □ Jehu A. Orr, "A Trip from Houston to Jackson, Miss., in 1845." Oxford, Mississippi: *Publications of the Mis-sissippi Historical Society,* Volume 9, 1906, pp. 174–176.

From Grenada our journey led us to Lexington, Yazoo City and Canton, and then to the capital. To properly appreciate a narrative of this trip and the strange scenes witnessed along the road we must understand what had been the financial condition of the country previous to that time. There were banks with capital stocks which ran into the millions, and in which the people placed infinite trust. They were headed by men whose financial integrity was unques-tioned; and yet, with all their money and strength, they were wrecked in the financial storm. . . .

It is a beautiful and fertile country through [these counties] . . . over which we traveled. Many plantations had been recently opened [before the depression], and on some of them elegant residences had been erected.

. . . The owners had freely indorsed for each other in the banks, and hun-dreds of thousands of dollars had been invested in negroes, brought from Vir-ginia and the Carolinas. When the storm broke over the banks the suits were so numerous in the courts that some of the lawyers had their declarations . . . printed by the quire, leaving blanks only for the names of the debtor, creditor and the amounts. In each of these counties an immense number of judgments had been obtained and the aggregate indebtedness had run into millions. A great number of these plantations in 1845 were uncultivated. The fences had fallen down, the homes and outhouses were tenantless and be-spoke widespread desolation. . . . We were told that as a general thing on the evening before abandonment those large plantations would present no unusual appearance. The stock would be in the stables, properly attended to; the cows would be in the cowpen; the hogs would be called and fed; the sheep would be herded; the plantation negroes would be in their proper places, and over all the hush of evening and the stillness of night would fall. On the morning following the smoke would curl from the chimneys, from residence and quarters, the cows would be lowing in the pen, the sheep bleating in the fold, the hogs in their place; not a wagon gone, not a vehicle missing; the meat left in the smokehouse, the poultry raising their usual disturbance—and not a human being, nor horse, nor mule, nor saddle, nor bridle on the whole place. Every negro, every horse, every mule spirited away in the darkness of the night—the negro women and children on horses and mules, the men on foot, all, all in a double-quick march for Texas, then a foreign government. The first object was to get across the county line, the next to cross the Mississippi River, and the next to cross the line of the Republic of Texas. All this had to be done before the executions could issue and be placed in the hands of the sheriffs of the different counties. Family carriages were left motionless to avoid creating any suspicion, the white families having taken their trips to neighboring towns, where the stage lines would convey them to points of safety—generally steamboat landings on the Mississippi—on their way to Texas. Even in the city of Columbus there remain on file in the circuit clerk's office printed declarations, containing not only the names of the plaintiff's banks, but in some cases the names of the defendants. This will convey an idea of the immense indebtedness to the banks of the country and of the universality of endorsements and personal securities. The immovable property was all that the executions could reach. After this came hundreds of suits by holders of bank notes.

V

A NEW ENGLAND REFORMER REACTS TO THE DEPRESSION

Orestes A. Brownson, a clergyman of Boston, was an associate of the socialist reformers Robert Owen, George Ripley, and Frances Wright. The following article indicates what some middle-class reformers thought should be done to relieve the plight of the working class during the "hungry forties." □ Orestes A. Brownson, "The Laboring Classes." *Boston Quarterly Review,* Volume 3, Number 11, July 1840, pp. 366–369, 375, 391–393.

No one can observe the signs of the times with much care, without perceiving that a crisis as to the relation of wealth and labor is approaching. . . .

We or our children will have to meet this crisis. The old war between the King and the Barons is well nigh ended, and so is that between the Barons and the Merchants and Manufacturers,—landed capital and commercial capital. The business man has become the peer of my Lord. And now commences the new struggle between the operative and his employer, between wealth and labor. Every day does this struggle . . . wax stronger and fiercer . . . .

. . . All over the world this fact stares us in the face, the workingman is poor and depressed, while a large portion of the non-workingmen, in the sense we now use the term, are wealthy. It may be laid down as a general rule, with but few exceptions, that men are rewarded in an inverse ratio to the amount of actual service they perform. Under every government on earth the largest salaries are annexed to those offices, which demand of their incumbents the least amount of actual labor . . . . The whole class of simple laborers are poor, and in general unable to procure any thing beyond the bare necessaries of life. . . .

. . . It is no pleasant thing to go days without food, to lie idle for weeks, seeking work and finding none, to rise in the morning with a wife and children you love, and know not where to procure them a breakfast, and to see constantly before you no brighter prospect than the almshouse. Yet these are no unfrequent incidents in the lives of our laboring population. Even in seasons of general prosperity, when there was only the ordinary cry of "hard times," we have seen hundreds of people in a . . . wealthy portion of our common country, suffering . . . , willing to work, and yet finding no work to do. . . .

The truth is, the evil we have pointed out is not merely individual in its character. It is not, in the case of any single individual, of any one man's procuring, nor can the efforts of any one man, directed solely to his own moral and religious perfection, do aught to remove it. What is purely individual in its nature, efforts of individuals to perfect themselves, may remove. But the evil we speak of is inherent in all our social arrangements, and cannot be cured without a radical change of those arrangements. Could we convert all men to Christianity in both theory and practice, as held by the most enlightened sect of Christians among us, the evils of the social state would remain untouched. Continue our present system of trade, and all its present evil consequences will follow, whether it be carried on by your best men or your worst. Put your best men, your wisest, most moral, and most religious men, at the head of your paper money banks, and the evils of the present banking system will remain scarcely diminished. The only way to get rid of its evils is to change the system, not its managers. . . .

Now the evils of which we have complained are of a social nature. That is, they have their root in the constitution of society as it is, and they have attained to their present growth by means of social influences, the action of government, of laws, and of systems and institutions upheld by society, and of which individuals are the slaves. This being the case, it is evident that they are to be removed only by the action of society, that is, by government, for the action of society is government.

But what shall government do? Its first doing must be an *un*doing. There has been thus far quite too much government, as well as government of the wrong kind. The first act of government we want, is a still further limitation of itself. It must begin by circumscribing within narrower limits its powers. And then it must proceed to repeal all laws which bear against the laboring classes, and then to enact such laws as are necessary to enable them to maintain their equality. We have no faith in those systems of elevating the working classes, which propose to elevate them without calling in the aid of the government. We must have government, and legislation expressly directed to this end.

. . . We want . . . legislation which shall free the government, whether State or Federal, from the control of the Banks. The Banks represent the interest of the employer, and therefore of necessity interests adverse to those of the employed; that is, they represent the interests of the business community in opposition to the laboring community. So long as the government remains under the control of the Banks, so long it must be in the hands of the natural enemies of the laboring classes, and may be made, nay, will be made, an instrument of depressing them yet lower. It is obvious then, that if our object be the elevation of the laboring classes, we must destroy the power of the Banks over the government, and place the government in the hands of the laboring classes themselves, or in the hands of those, if such there be, who have an identity of interest with them. But this cannot be done so long as the Banks exist. Such is the subtle influence of credit, and such the power of capital, that a banking system like ours, if sustained, necessarily and inevitably becomes the real and efficient government of the country. . . . Uncompromising hostility to the whole banking system should therefore be the motto of every working man, and of every friend of humanity. The system must be destroyed. On this point . . . [there] must be no misgiving, no subterfuge, no palliation. The system is at war with the rights and interests of labor, and it must go. . . .

Following the destruction of the Banks, must come that of all monopolies, of all PRIVILEGE. There are many of these. We cannot specify them all; we therefore select only one, the greatest of them all, the privilege which some have of being born rich while others are born poor. It will be seen at once that we allude to the hereditary descent of property, an anomaly in our American system which must be removed, or the system itself will be destroyed.

PROBLEM *5*

The Causes of the Depression:
An Interpretation

Prosperity returned to the nation in the mid-1840's. Cotton prices rose again and with them prosperity returned to the South. Foreigners once more looked favorably upon America as a place to invest funds. The flow of capital across the Atlantic helped to revitalize trade, improve the transportation network, and spur industry. Immigrants, particularly from Ireland, arrived by the thousands, providing a new source of labor and creating new demands for the products of field and factory. The depression was over, though its memory remained in the hearts of the men and women who had suffered through it.

The first four Problems in Unit One have traced the course of American economic history during the 1830's and the 1840's. Many of the readings are short explicit interpretations of the causes of the depression. Others imply an interpretation by the way the authors arranged evidence or by their choice of topics. Problem 5 has interpretation as its focus. It consists of three accounts of the causes of the depression, two of them from contemporaries, and the third from a modern historian.

The interpretation of an event as complicated as a depression involves a large number of factors rather than a single cause which can be easily isolated and identified. Moreover, the interpretation of events in economic history calls for a knowledge of economic analysis which is often expressed in mathematical terms by professional economists. Even without a knowledge of economic theory, however, the student of history can understand most of the issues on which historians have had divided opinions in the past.

Each of the three excerpts in Problem 5 presents an interpretation of the cause of the depression of the 1830's and 1840's. The first two, by Henry Clay and Martin Van Buren, were written during the depression by men who were deeply involved in the measures they were describing. They benefit from the advantages and suffer from the handicaps of being close to the events of the times. The third reading, a modern version, has the advantage of more than a hundred years of hindsight. As you read these interpretations, keep the following questions in mind:

1   Each of the three accounts isolates certain circumstances as the major causes of the depression. What are the basic elements of disagreement? Why do the authors disagree so much?

2   Which interpretation, if any, does the material in the first four Problems best support?

3   Clay insists "the people are not to blame" for the depression. Is his viewpoint simply the expression of a politician? Can the public be exonerated in an economic collapse?

I

HENRY CLAY ANALYZES THE CAUSES OF THE DEPRESSION

During the winter of 1839 and 1840 the subject of the depression was uppermost in the minds of politicians. Henry Clay, the leading Whig statesman in the Senate, sensed a victory for his party in the coming election and presented its position in this speech addressed to President Martin Van Buren. ☐ Daniel Mallory, Editor, *The Life and Speeches of the Hon. Henry Clay,* Volume 2, pp. 385–386. New York: Robert P. Bixby and Company, copyright © 1843.

Mr. President, it is no less the duty of the statesman than of the physician to ascertain the exact state of the body to which he is to minister before he ventures to prescribe any healing remedy. It is with no pleasure, but with profound regret, that I survey the present condition of our country . . . . [The] people are surrounded with difficulties, greatly embarrassed, and involved in debt. . . . Property is falling in value; all the great staples of the country are declining in price, and destined, I fear, to further decline. . . . The banks are rapidly decreasing the amount of their circulation. About one half of them, extending from New Jersey to the extreme southwest, have suspended specie payments, presenting an image of a paralytic . . . . The banks are without a head; and instead of union, concert, and coöperation between them, we behold jealousy, distrust, and enmity. We have no currency whatever possessing uniform value throughout the whole country. That which we have, consisting almost entirely of the issues of banks, is in a state of the utmost disorder, insomuch that it varies, in comparison with the specie standard, from par to fifty per centum discount. Exchanges, too, are in the greatest possible confusion; not merely between distant parts of the union, but between cities and places in the same neighborhood . . . . The products of our agricultural industry are unable to find their way to market from the want of means in the hands of traders to purchase them, or from the want of confidence in the stability of things; many of our manufactories stopped or stopping, especially in the important branch of woollens; and a vast accumulation of their fabrics on hand, owing to the destruction of confidence, and the wretched state of exchange between different sections of the union.

. . . If the present unhappy state of our country had been brought upon the people by their folly and extravagance, it ought to be borne with fortitude, and without complaint, and without reproach. But it is my deliberate judgment that it has not been; that the people are not to blame, and that the principal causes of existing embarrassments are not to be traced to them. . . . I believe our pecuniary distresses have mainly sprung from the refusal to recharter the late bank of the United States; the removal of the public deposits from that institution; the multiplication of state banks in consequence, and the treasury stimulus given to them to extend their operations; the bungling manner in which the law depositing the surplus treasure with the states was executed; the treasury circular; and, although last, perhaps not least, the exercise of the power of the veto on the bill for distributing among the states the net proceeds of the sale of the public lands.

What, Mr. President, is needed, at the present crisis, to restore the prosperity of the people? A sound local currency, mixed with a currency possessing uniform value throughout the whole country, a reëstablishment of regular exchanges between different parts of the union, and a revival of general confidence.

The people want, in short, good government at Washington, the abandonment of rash and ruinous experiments, the practice here of economy, and the pursuit of the safe lights of experience. Give us these, and the growth of our population, the enterprise of our people, and the abundance, variety, and richness of the products of our soil, and of our industry, with the blessing of Providence, will carry us triumphantly through all our complicated embarrassments.

II

VAN BUREN LOOKS IN ANOTHER DIRECTION

In his third annual message to Congress on December 2, 1839, President Martin Van Buren placed the depression in a world setting. He commented about the role which he thought the federal government should play in the economic crisis. ☐ James D. Richardson, Compiler, *Messages and Papers of the Presidents, 1789–1897,* Volume 3, pp. 542–545, 553. Washington, D.C.: Authority of Congress. Copyright © 1897 by James D. Richardson.

Scarcely were the country and Government relieved in a degree from the difficulties occasioned by the general suspension of 1837 when a partial one, occurring within thirty months of the former, produced new and serious embarrassments . . . . There was nothing in the condition of the country to endanger a well-managed banking institution; commerce was deranged by no foreign war; every branch of manufacturing industry was crowned with rich rewards, and the more than usual abundance of our harvests, after supplying our domestic wants, had left our granaries and storehouses filled with a surplus for exportation. It is in the midst of this that an irredeemable and depreciated paper currency is entailed upon the people . . . .

New dangers to the banks are . . . daily disclosed from the extension of that system of extravagant credit of which they are the pillars. Formerly our foreign commerce was principally founded on an exchange of commodities, including the precious metals, and leaving in its transactions but little foreign debt. Such is not now the case. Aided by the facilities afforded by the banks, mere credit has become too commonly the basis of trade. . . . The disasters attendant on this deviation from the former course of business in this country are now shared alike by banks and individuals to an extent of which there is perhaps no previous example in the annals of our country. So long as a willingness of the foreign lender and a sufficient export of our productions . . . leave the flow of credit undisturbed all appears to 'be prosperous, but as soon as it is checked by any hesitation abroad or by an inability to make payment . . . [,] the evils of the system are disclosed. . . .

Nor is it to be overlooked that there exists a chain of necessary dependence among these institutions which obliges them to a great extent to follow the course of others, notwithstanding its injustice to their own immediate creditors or injury to the particular community in which they are placed. This dependence of a bank . . . is not merely on others in its own vicinity, but on all those which connect it with the center of trade. Distant banks may fail without seriously affecting those in our principal commercial cities, but the failure of the latter is felt at the extremities of the Union. . . .

But this chain of dependence does not stop here. It does not terminate at Philadelphia or New York. It reaches across the ocean and ends in London, the center of the credit system. The same laws of trade which give to the banks in our principal cities power over the whole banking system of the United States subject the former, in their turn, to the money power in Great Britain. . . .

From this influence they can not now entirely escape, for it has its origin in the credit currencies of the two countries; it is strengthened by the current of trade and exchange which centers in London, and is rendered almost irresistible by the large debts contracted there by our merchants, our banks, and our States. . . . It is not by the increase of this debt that relief is to be sought. . . . If we would escape embarrassment, public and private, we must cease to run in debt except for objects of necessity or such as will yield a certain return. . . . By ceasing to run in debt and applying the surplus of our crops and incomes to the discharge of existing obligations, buying less and selling more, and managing all affairs, public and private, with strict economy and frugality, we shall see our country soon recover from a temporary depression, arising not from natural and permanent causes, but from those I have enumerated, and advance with renewed vigor in her career of prosperity.

III

"THE UNDERLYING FORCES"

Douglass C. North of the University of Washington, and an editor of the *Journal of Economic History,* made a study of the causes of the Panic of 1837 and the ensuing depression. In discussing this financial disaster, North sees the causes in a different light from that of the men of the 1830's and 1840's. ☐ Douglass C. North, *The Economic Growth of the United States, 1790–1860,* pp. 198–203. Englewood Cliffs, New Jersey: Prentice-Hall, Inc., copyright © 1961.

The era of expansion between 1831 and 1839 may be summarized as follows: The initial expansion was set off by the conjunction of rising cotton prices and the structural changes in the three regions brought about by the development of regional interdependence.

[The three regions are the Northeast, the Old Northwest, and the South. The structural changes were mainly those arising from manufacturing, commercial services, and finance in the Northeast; cereal crop agriculture in the Northwest; and cotton in the South.]

. . . [Expansion] took place at first with scant rise in prices . . . . Once under way, the actual or anticipated development of internal improvements implied a reduction in transfer [or transportation] costs, making it possible for vast new areas to market their commodities and accelerate further the westward movement and demand for land. Bank expansion played the most important role in supplying capital; foreign investment was selective and limited. The significant flow of foreign funds came later . . . .

The growth of facilities to market these commodities and supply the local needs of planters or settlers in new areas led to a construction boom. This expansion reacted in turn on the East in the form of demand for services and manufactured goods. The . . . widening of the market permitted greater specialization and increased efficiency in manufacturing. The inflow of capital sustained the expansion for a number of years . . . .

This brief summary focuses upon the underlying real forces . . . but neglects the . . . economic influences which affected the pace and timing of expansion and subsequent contraction. . . .

The disparity in English and American price levels, the flow of specie, and the speculation in America combined as the forces underlying the Panic of 1837. That spring was a dismal one in economic affairs. Sterling bills sold at a 12.5 per cent premium, domestic credit was severely restricted, and innumerable banks and commercial establishments failed. General suspension of specie payments went into effect in May. . . .

The Panic of 1837 was an interruption and not an end to the underlying expansive forces in the economy. The sharp drop in cotton prices reflected the readjustment in the American price level rather than any larger increase in supply as a result of new lands being put into cultivation. By the spring of 1838, cotton prices were again rising, the low point having been reached in early summer of 1837, and economic expansion was visible on all sides. The improving profitability of cotton and western staples again attracted foreign capital into plantation expansion and *productive* internal improvements. The revival of western regional expansion and the cotton trade provided the necessary stimulus for expansion of manufacturing in the East. Both domestic wholesale prices and export prices rose sharply.

The Second Bank, which had now become the United States Bank of

Pennsylvania, began its celebrated (or notorious) speculation in cotton in July 1837 . . . . The decline in cotton prices plummeted from a high of 17 cents a pound in April 1839 at Charleston to 7½ cents a pound a year later. The results were disastrous, and not only for the Bank. They also ushered in a depression . . . . It was not merely the overexpansion of cotton, nor even the tremendous increase in capacity of western foodstuffs, which depressed prices. It was these factors in conjunction with the credit structure and the cessation of foreign investment, plus the necessary readjustment in American price levels vis-à-vis foreign prices, which triggered the depression. The difference between 1837 and 1839 was that the former panic had centered around temporary maladjustments in internal monetary affairs and external influences, while these monetary and external influences in the latter period were combined with the real effects of a decade of uninhibited expansion of productive capacity, which necessarily entailed a long period of readjustment.

. . . There was a precipitous decline [from 1839 to 1843] in domestic and export prices, a cessation of capital imports, and the return of securities to the United States as Pennsylvania, Maryland and other states defaulted on their interest payments. Both domestic and foreign trade declined sharply, with the West and South the hardest hit. The cessation of capital imports halted the vast program of internal improvements and accompanying investments in the economic opportunities associated with a new region. The stoppage of the flow of capital into the West from the Northeast operated on the West in much the same way that it operated between the United States and England. During the period of capital inflow, western prices rose relative to those of the Northeast, but when this inflow ceased the readjustment in western price levels meant a more drastic decline than for the economy as a whole. The same pattern held for the South, except that the fall in cotton prices was even more severe. Cotton planters had little incentive to expand production, and as the price continued to drop the advantage of becoming more self-sufficient by putting available acreage into corn and hogs became evident. While the depression did not spare the Northeast and was perhaps harder on states like Pennsylvania, with large commitments in internal improvements, the decline in manufacturing prices was relatively less than that of agricultural products . . . .

The precipitous price decline of 1839 leveled off, and prices actually rose slightly in late 1840 and 1841. Then the decline resumed, continuing until the beginning of 1843. By 1843, the depression had run its course, foreign and domestic price levels were in line, and a new era of expansion was slowly getting under way. But cotton was no longer king.

unit two

The Depression of 1893-1898

For almost fifty years after 1844 the United States experienced a series of ups and downs in its economy, with serious low points in 1857, in the late 1870's, and again in 1884. None were so serious, however, as the depression that hit the country in 1893 after several years of relative prosperity. At the worst periods of the depression, in 1894 and in 1896, economic activity declined about 25 per cent. Recovery began in 1897, but most industries were not working at capacity again until 1901 and some did not recover completely until 1907. This economic strain caused widespread social unrest and led to one of the most bitter political struggles in United States history.

A panic which began to develop in February 1893 when the Reading Railroad went bankrupt ushered in the depression. The effect of the Reading bankruptcy was somewhat offset by President Grover Cleveland's inauguration and a belief among members of the business community that the President would "maintain our national credit and avert financial disaster." However, failures among smaller financial and industrial firms developed and grew in number. Then, on May 5, the supposedly solid National Cordage Company failed and brought about a stock market collapse and the panic. By the end of 1893 some 500 banks and 16,000 business firms had been financially ruined.

Following the panic the country settled into a deep depression. All indicators of economic activity showed marked declines. Not until 1897 did the economy return to the level of 1892, and another five years passed before people generally agreed that prosperity had returned. In the period between 1894 and early 1897 unemployment varied between 20 and 15 per cent, high enough to be socially and politically dangerous.

Without doubt the farmers suffered most from the depression of the 1890's. Even in the years of prosperity farming had become a declining industry, and during the 1890's farmers were faced with disaster, particularly in the Middle Western states. Their misfortunes were reflected in other areas and among other groups, for farmers had become bound, through a new transportation and communication network, with almost every wage-earner, merchant, manufacturer, and banker. All of them felt the eco-

nomic disruption. Such was the price the nation paid for its new status as a great industrial power.

The Problems in Unit Two explore the causes of the depression of the 1890's and examine its effects. Problem 6 presents evidence in statistical form about the economy and challenges the student to develop hypotheses about it. Problem 7 describes the development of a national economy during the second half of the nineteenth century and sets the stage for an understanding of the widespread effects of the depression. Problem 8 analyzes the situation of the farmer, and Problem 9 examines the role of government during the depression. Problem 10 presents an interpretation of the depression by a modern historian.

PROBLEM 6

A View of the Economy in the 1890's

Many Americans in the 1890's believed that the national economy was stable and secure. Yet, in spite of widespread optimism a severe depression began in 1893 and lasted almost until the turn of the century. Could the depression have been averted? There were those who thought so if one or two malpractices in the economy could have been corrected. Some critics blamed business and industry, claiming that workers' wages had not been increased fast enough to provide the purchasing power necessary to buy the goods and services required to keep the factories working. The federal government came in for its share of blame. Businessmen, farmers, and miners claimed that if the government had increased the amount of money in circulation, consumer purchasing power would have been able to keep pace with the production of goods. Whatever the cause of the depression, it was a national calamity. A look at the statistical data for the 1890's will help you form some hypotheses about the causes, extent, and duration of the depression of the nineties.

What are hypotheses, and how do historians form them? In interpreting and understanding the depression of the 1890's—or any historical event—the historian has to find the facts and then discover how the facts are related. A tentative statement of relationship between two or more facts is a hypothesis.

You can see how this process works by using the facts about agricultural production which are given in Table 1.

SOME STATISTICS ABOUT AGRICULTURE

TABLE 1

Year	Production of wheat *in millions of bushels*	Price of wheat per bushel[1] *in dollars*	Production of cotton *in millions of bales*	Price of cotton per pound[1] *in dollars*
1889	504.4	$ .698	7.5	$ .09
1890	449.0	.837	8.7	.09
1891	677.5	.831	9.0	.07
1892	611.9	.624	6.7	.08
1893	505.8	.534	7.5	.07
1894	541.9	.489	9.9	.05
1895	542.1	.505	7.2	.08
1896	523.0	.721	8.5	.07
1897	606.2	.809	10.9	.07
1898	768.1	.579	11.3	.06
1899	655.1	.588	9.3	.07
1900	599.3	.621	10.1	.09

Historical Statistics, pp. 297, 301–302.
[1]Current prices.

On the basis of these data, what happened to the income of farmers in the period 1890 to 1895? Your answer to this question is a hypothesis. It is a beginning point of research and inquiry. More evidence is needed before the hypothesis can be accepted as truth—and therefore useful—or rejected as false.

Now can you make a hypothesis that would relate farm income to prosperity of factory workers? For example, would wheat farmers be likely to buy new machinery in 1894?

This activity is a sample of the kind you will carry out in Problem 6. It is important to understand that the questions asked do not have right or wrong answers. You will have an opportunity to test your hypothesis as more evidence is added in the readings in this Unit.

As you study Problem 6 and form hypotheses, keep these questions in mind:

1   How were the various sectors of the economy (agriculture, industry, finance) related to one another in the 1890's? Did the cycle of prosperity and depression in one sector parallel the cycle in another?

2   Could anything have been done to prevent the depression or to lessen its impact on the American people?

SOME STATISTICS OF THE NINETIES

All tables, including Table 1 on page 60, unless otherwise credited, are from a volume prepared by the Bureau of the Census, with the advice and assistance of the Committee on Historical Statistics. The pages from which the tables are taken are shown with the tables. □ *Historical Statistics of the United States: Colonial Times to 1957.* Washington, D.C.: United States Bureau of the Census, 1960.

STEEL, RAILROADS, AND MANUFACTURING

The five columns of Table 2 show the activity in three major parts of the American economy—basic steel production, the railroad industry, and manufacturing in general. The railroad industry constituted the big business of the 1890's.

1   Is there a relationship among activities in these three parts of the economy?

2   What hypothesis can you make relating the data from Table 2 to that in Table 1?

TABLE 2

Year	Steel production *in millions of long tons*	Rails produced *in millions of long tons*	Locomotives produced *number*	Freight cars produced *number*	Index of manufacturing production[1]
1889	3.4	1.5	1,860	70,600	66
1890	4.3	1.9	2,300	103,800	71
1891	3.9	1.3	2,165	95,500	73
1892	4.9	1.6	2,012	98,100	79
1893	4.0	1.1	2,011	56,900	70
1894	4.4	1.0	695	17,000	68
1895	6.1	1.3	1,101	38,100	81
1896	5.3	1.1	1,175	51,200	74
1897	7.2	1.6	1,251	43,600	80
1898	8.9	2.0	1,875	99,800	91
1899	10.6	2.3	2,475	119,900	100
1900	10.2	2.4	3,153	115,600	100

Historical Statistics, pp. 409, 416.
[1] 1899 = 100.

ANNUAL WAGES AND SALARIES

There can be no doubt that the effects of the depression of the nineties were felt in every village and city. Farmers and factory workers suffered. But workers in some jobs were apparently not affected—indeed, their income increased.

Table 3 shows the annual wages and salaries of workers in nine occupations.

1 Which types of jobs showed the greatest fluctuation in wage and salary? How can you account for the differences between those producing goods (manufacturing and industrial employees) and those producing services?

2 Do the wage and salary data in Table 3 follow the same pattern as the agriculture and industry data in Tables 1 and 2?

TABLE 3 - Part A

Year	Manufacturing	Steam railroads	Street railways	Gas and electricity
1890	$ 439	$ 560	$ 557	$ 687
1891	442	554	529	587
1892	446	563	535	625
1893	420	563	526	627
1894	386	546	508	670
1895	416	546	509	640
1896	406	544	531	665
1897	408	543	552	703
1898	412	542	558	698
1899	426	543	591	612

TABLE 3 — Part B

Year	Clerical workers	Bituminous coal mining	Farm labor	Postal employees	Public school teachers
1890	$ 848	$ 406	$ 233	$ 878	$ 256
1891	882	377	236	894	264
1892	885	393	238	899	270
1893	923	383	232	902	276
1894	928	292	214	919	283
1895	941	307	216	935	289
1896	954	282	220	944	294
1897	970	270	224	950	298
1898	1,010	316	228	939	306
1899	1,004	379	239	924	318

Historical Statistics, pp. 91–92.

NATIONAL BANKS AND COMMERCIAL BUSINESSES

Table 4 gives some data about national banks and business in general. Net earnings are the profits made by the banks.

1 According to the table, when did bank profits decline sharply? When was the number of business failures highest?

2 Did the changes in bank prosperity parallel those in farming and manufacturing? What does this table tell you about the economy?

TABLE 4

Year	National banks		Commercial businesses	
	Number of banks	Net earnings	Number of business concerns	Rate of business failures
		in millions of dollars	*in thousands*	*per 10,000 concerns*
1889	3,239	$ 86.	1,051.1	103
1890	3,484	93.	1,110.6	99
1891	3,652	96.	1,143.0	107
1892	3,759	90.	1,172.7	89
1893	3,807	91.	1,193.1	130
1894	3,770	80.	1,114.2	123
1895	3,715	75.	1,209.3	112
1896	3,689	81.	1,151.6	133
1897	3,610	77.	1,058.5	125
1898	3,582	81.	1,105.8	111
1899	3,583	88.	1,147.6	82
1900	3,732	121.	1,174.0	92

Historical Statistics, pp. 570, 638.

UNITED STATES MONEY SUPPLY

People carry on business with money. Thus, the historian studying the economic health of the nation is tremendously interested in the money supply. Money consists of coins and currency and of checking accounts, called demand deposits.

During the late 1870's and through the 1880's, silver miners, farmers, and labor groups wanted the federal government to buy and coin unlimited amounts of silver. In 1890 the Sherman Silver Purchase Act was passed. It required the federal government to increase its purchase of silver by 100 per cent and to issue currency that could be redeemed in either silver or gold.

In the early 1890's the government was already suffering from heavy gold withdrawals. Foreign creditors had to be paid in gold. Furthermore, an increasing number of pension grants to Union army veterans between 1889 and 1893 drew heavily on the gold reserve. The redemption of silver certificates for gold created a greater drain on the reserve than the government could sustain. As a result of the strain on its gold reserve, the government was reluctant to issue more money. It was said to have a "tight-money" policy— a policy thought by some to have had an effect on the economy.

Some critics of the time even went so far as to suggest the tight-money supply was a cause of the depression. When money is in short supply, interest rates rise; businessmen hesitate to borrow. Thus, the effect of a tight-money policy may be to discourage the investment necessary to keep the economy healthy and expanding. Table 5 shows figures on the United States money supply from 1892 to 1900.

1 Did the total supply of money increase significantly during the worst years of the depression?

2 From the data in the last column of Table 5, does the volume of money alone appear to be responsible for the depression?

TABLE 5

Year	Currency and coins in millions of dollars	Demand deposits in millions of dollars	Total volume of money including savings in millions of dollars
1892	$ 1,015	$ 2,880	$ 5,824
1893	1,081	2,766	5,854
1894	972	2,807	5,773
1895	971	2,960	6,019
1896	974	2,839	6,033
1897	1,013	2,871	6,189
1898	1,150	3,432	6,979
1899	1,181	4,162	7,960
1900	1,331	4,420	8,766

Historical Statistics, p. 646.

ESTIMATED ANNUAL POPULATION AND IMMIGRATION

The rapid increase in population was a major force in the economic growth of the United States after 1865. Serious declines in the economy were always marked by a decrease in the rate of population growth.

1 What happened to the total population during the 1890's according to Table 6? to the rate of immigration? to percentage of increase in population? Do these three sets of data suggest a relationship between depression and birth rate?

2 Why might a decline in the rate of population growth intensify a depression that was already underway? Would such a decline affect the number of new houses built? the rate at which new factories were built?

TABLE 6

Year	Estimated total population	Estimated total immigration	Annual percentage increase in population
1890	63,056,000	455,302	2.12
1891	64,361,000	560,319	2.06
1892	65,666,000	579,663	2.03
1893	66,970,000	439,730	2.0
1894	68,275,000	285,631	1.98
1895	69,580,000	258,536	1.92

TABLE 6 – Continued

Year	Estimated total population	Estimated total immigration	Annual percentage increase in population
1896	70,885,000	343,267	1.88
1897	72,189,000	230,832	1.86
1898	73,494,000	229,299	1.81
1899	74,799,000	311,715	1.78
1900	76,094,000	448,572	1.75
1901	77,585,000	487,918	1.95
1902	79,160,000	648,743	2.02

Historical Statistics, pp. 7, 56.

FEDERAL REVENUE AND EXPENDITURE

One way to judge government response to a depression is to observe the changes in government revenue and expenditure. Many modern economists argue that government may be able to check a depression by spending additional money to spur employment. Workers hired and paid by government funds will have money to purchase goods and services which may in turn improve the prosperity of private business.

1   Judging by the figures in Table 7, did the government increase expenditure during the worst years of the depression? On the other hand, did government cut expenditure far enough to balance the budget?

2   What relationship do you find between the statistics on unemployment and government expenditure from 1889 to 1900?

TABLE 7

Year	Government revenue in millions of dollars	Government expenditure in millions of dollars	Surplus (+) Deficit (−)[1] in millions of dollars	Percentage of estimated unemployment in manufacturing, transportation[2]
1890	$ 403.1	$ 318.0	$ +85.1	5.1
1891	392.6	365.8	+26.8	5.6
1892	354.9	345.0	+ 9.9	3.7
1893	385.8	383.5	+ 2.3	9.6
1894	306.4	367.5	− 61.1	16.7
1895	324.7	356.2	− 31.5	11.9
1896	338.1	352.2	− 14.1	15.3
1897	347.7	365.8	− 18.1	14.5
1898	405.3	443.4	− 38.1	13.9
1899	516.0	605.1	− 89.1	7.7
1900	567.2	520.9	+46.3	6.3

Historical Statistics, pp. 712, 718.
[1] Calculated from columns showing government revenue and expenditure.
[2] Douglas, Paul H., *Real Wages in the United States, 1890–1926,* p. 440. New York: Houghton, Mifflin Company, 1930. Copyright, 1930, by the Pollak Foundation for Economic Research. Used by permission.

ESTIMATES OF GROSS NATIONAL PRODUCT

The term *Gross National Product,* or *GNP,* is the total market value of all goods and services produced in an economy. The best overall indication of the growth or decline of an economy is the annual change in its Gross National Product. The best overall indication of how effective an economic system is in providing the people with an improving standard of living is *Gross National Product per capita.*

The term *Net capital formation* means investments, such as additions to equipment, tools, and buildings.

Flow of goods to consumers includes all goods and services, paid for and consumed or used by households.

1   GNP shows a drop in only one year and increases in all the others, while GNP per capita shows a drop in two years. Do the data in Table 6 help you develop a hypothesis to account for this variation?

2   During the 1890's net investment in new capital (net capital formation) tended to rise and fall by a larger proportion than did purchases by consumers (flow of goods to consumers). This situation is typical of all modern depressions. Can you think of any reasons why it happens? As you formulate your hypothesis, you may wish to refer again to Tables 1, 2, 4, and 6.

TABLE 8

Year	GNP[1] in billions of dollars	GNP per capita[2] in dollars	Net capital formation[1] in billions of dollars	Flow of goods to consumers[1] in billions of dollars
1889	$ 12.0	$ 195	$ 1.13	$ 9.59
1890	12.4	195	1.86	9.25
1891	12.9	200	1.73	9.91
1892	13.3	200	2.23	9.76
1893	13.3	200	1.56	10.3
1894	12.0	180	1.33	9.30
1895	12.9	185	1.60	9.95
1896	12.9	180	1.43	10.1
1897	13.9	190	1.71	10.7
1898	14.8	200	1.80	11.4
1899	16.4	225	2.00	12.5
1900	17.9	235	2.48	13.5

[1]Kuznets, Simon, *Capital in the American Economy,* p. 557. Princeton, New Jersey: Princeton University Press. Copyright © 1961 by National Bureau of Economic Research, Inc. Used by permission.
[2]Figures for GNP per capita were calculated by dividing estimated annual GNP by estimated annual population (Table 6).

PROBLEM 7

The Rise of a National Economy

During the first half of the nineteenth century there were really three economies within the United States. Most Americans still lived within a family economy, growing their own food and making most of what they needed for shelter and clothing. Increasing numbers of people also participated in local economies, selling some goods in nearby towns and buying essential supplies in return. Only a relatively few were affected by transactions in the national and international economies. They made goods or raised crops primarily for sale in the market and bought almost all the products they consumed.

Because so small a number of Americans were involved in the national and the international economies, depressions during the early nineteenth century touched only part of the people seriously. Many a small farmer weathered the crisis of the 1840's without undue suffering. He continued to raise his own food, to provide his own clothing, and to build his own shelter.

All of those hardest hit, such as owners of cotton plantations, were involved in the national or international economies, but disaster for one group of producers did not necessarily mean hard times for all.

This situation had changed rapidly by the 1870's. More and more farmers became involved in the market. Instead of raising crops by hand to provide for their families, they bought machines and raised one or two large crops for the market, purchasing almost everything they needed with the proceeds. This process built ties among field, factory, and counting house. The rapid spread of the railroad network indicates how quickly these ties were being forged. The welfare of the farms had become linked to the welfare of the rest of the country. In an economy joined by bonds of trade, a collapse in one area has repercussions everywhere.

By the 1890's the interdependence of the elements of the American economy was even more obvious. Problem 7 traces this interdependence and hints at its implications for American society. As you·read Problem 7, you may wish to look again at the statistics in Problem 6. In addition, keep the following questions in mind:

1   What developments account for the integration of the national economy in the late nineteenth century?

2   What did the growth of the number and the proportion of people involved in the national and international economies imply for American society?

3   Why would a depression in the 1890's be likely to have a deeper impact than a similar downturn fifty years previously?

LINKING THE ECONOMY TOGETHER

Samuel P. Hays, Chairman of the Department of History at the University of Pittsburgh, discusses the development of a national economy in the selection which follows. □ Samuel P. Hays, *The Response to Industrialism, 1885–1914*, pp. 4–17. Chicago: University of Chicago Press, copyright © 1957.

In the United States in the nineteenth century many factors favored industrial growth. Abundant resources, high in quality and exploitable with relatively small amounts of labor and capital, lay waiting to be developed. Industry could draw a large and cheap labor supply from a reservoir of peasants in Europe who eagerly responded when they learned of American economic opportunities. Domestic capital, derived from earlier mercantile enterprise, provided funds essential for the nation's internal development; European capital augmented domestic savings especially in mining, railroads, and banks. Enterprisers in the United States, moreover, faced few political barriers to economic exchange; the Constitution prohibited states from imposing restrictions on interstate commerce and thereby promoted combination of the factors of production over a vast and varied geographical area. Finally, pre-industrial America had developed a capable group of entrepreneurs; though experienced chiefly in organizing commerce, they were eager to take advantage of every opportunity to expand their operations. The American people displayed a vigorous spirit of enterprise notably in the North, which boasted of its "Yankee ingenuity."

A nationwide transportation system constructed between 1820 and 1915 enabled Americans to exploit fully these latent factors of economic growth. The success of the Erie Canal in New York and the development of the steamboat set off a craze of canal building in the 1820's and initiated a revolution in transportation and communication. Railroads, first constructed in the 1830's, soon surpassed the canals in importance. Although slowed momentarily by the Civil War, railroad expansion proceeded with great rapidity between 1868 and the depression of 1893. Construction was limited to the area east of the Mississippi prior to the Civil War but expanded to the Pacific Coast in the 1870's and 1880's. In the industrial Northeast new mileage produced an extremely dense and complex network. . . .

Railroad mileage grew rapidly because Americans in all walks of life visualized the economic progress that cheap transportation could set in motion. Merchants in thriving communities and in communities which hoped to thrive endeavored to reach wider markets by extending their transportation facilities. Before the Civil War, merchants of each of the major Atlantic seaports . . . promoted competitive railroad building . . . . The search for markets generated hundreds of similar projects throughout the country. Frequently they were financed through bond and stock subscriptions raised either from merchants themselves or from the general public in campaigns which local commercial associations promoted. Farmers eagerly joined in the crusade; they, too, contributed personal savings and often mortgaged their farms to raise funds to speed construction. Whole communities . . . participated in the mania. . . .

Cheap, rapid transportation brought all sectors of the economy into close contact with one another; factors of production could be combined far more readily than before. Previously, for example, high shipment costs often prohibited the combination of iron ore and coal located scarcely ten miles apart; but now the economic distance between such resources was phenomenally reduced. Canals and steamboats lowered river-transport costs to less than a tenth of land travel. Initially railroads did not lower rates further between points served by waterways; but they were faster than steamboats, were free from ice and low-water barriers, and penetrated to areas which water carriers could not possibly reach.

These efficiencies stimulated economic growth not only by reducing the cost of production but even more significantly by creating a national market; the transportation and communications revolution destroyed barriers to distribution and permitted producers to sell to consumers throughout the nation. For example, the local blacksmith's plowshares, kettles, pots, and pans before the transportation revolution cost less than similar items manufactured fifty miles away and subject to high shipping charges. Manufacturers were excluded from every distant market, but within their own locality enjoyed a monopoly. Railroads in particular now eliminated these exclusive markets; they opened every part of the country to the producers of modern industry and by stimulating mass consumption greatly encouraged the growth of mass production.

No less important . . . was rapid nationwide communication. The telegraph was first successfully operated in 1844 by Samuel F. B. Morse (1791-1872), a New England artist turned inventor. Widely used during the Civil War, it co-ordinated the myriad transactions of a growing economy as effectively as it aided military operations. While the telegraph speeded communications over longer distances, the telephone, patented by Alexander Graham Bell (1847-1922) in 1876, replaced messengers in the mushrooming urban centers and speeded the complex administrative processes necessary for large-scale industrial management.

The modern press, though less spectacular, was equally vital in co-ordinating the intricate functions of the new economy. Technical innovations, such as the rotary press (1875), enormously increased the output and lowered the cost of newspaper production. Nationwide advertising . . . brought producer and consumer together with a speed previously impossible. The new communication supplemented the new transportation in creating the highly integrated and complex human relationships inherent in modern industrialism.

Railroad construction in the latter half of the nineteenth century served as the most important direct stimulant to production. Lumber mills, quarries, ironworks, and carriage factories found a rapidly growing market in railways. The railroad-construction labor force reached 200,000 in the boom of the 1880's. The new roads, moreover, were major users of both domestic and foreign capital. The close correspondence between the ups and downs of new construction and nationwide economic fluctuations in the post-Civil War era provided evidence of the all-pervasive impact of the railroad on the entire economy. A loss of confidence in railroads affected the money market so as to trigger the depressions of 1873, 1884, and 1893.

The rapidly expanding iron and steel industry, stimulated enormously by the railroads, became the foundation of industrial America. Far outstripping the domestic supply, the need for iron and steel constantly encouraged expansion of American mills. By 1850 railroads had become the leading industrial market for iron, and by 1875 railroad construction, reconstruction, and maintenance consumed over half of the iron produced in the United States. The demand for railroad iron, moreover, brought about the all-important technological shift from charcoal to coke in iron production. Before the introduction of the steam locomotive, rural blacksmiths, who purchased most of the iron, preferred a charcoal-manufactured product which they could work more easily than iron smelted with coal. Coal-smelted iron was quite satisfactory for structural shapes, rails, and locomotives. Coke-produced iron, moreover, permitted a mass production of iron previously not practical. The heavy cost of . . . [transporting] wood for charcoal limited the size of the area from which fuel could be feasibly drawn, and consequently the size of the blast furnace. But the enormous coal fields of western Pennsylvania presented no such limitations; in a relatively small geographical area they provided the fuel essential for large-scale production. Once the new railroad market appeared, therefore, coke replaced charcoal, and huge blast furnaces and rolling mills grew rapidly in the new capital of the iron industry at Pittsburgh. . . .

Railroads, then, both lowered the cost of transportation and stimulated the economy directly by their use of labor, capital, and iron. They also created the mass markets that made mass production possible. When markets were local and limited in size, there was no incentive for businessmen to produce in larger amounts to realize the resultant savings in costs. But the unlimited possibilities of the new mass markets stimulated entrepreneurs to explore and develop mass-production techniques. In the iron and steel industry, for example, the size and scope of production increased rapidly: the average daily output of a blast furnace increased from . . . 45 tons before the Civil War to more than 400 tons in the early twentieth century. Mass production was introduced in many other fields as well, notably lumbering, flour milling, meat packing, and textile manufacturing. For example, larger and more efficient saws were adopted in the lumber industry, and in the milling industry the rolling process, first used extensively in Minneapolis, increased both the output and the quality of flour.

Mass production also depended upon improved techniques, of which standardization of parts and processes was especially significant. Repetitive production of a standard item, independent of the vagaries of the individual craftsman, was the heart of the technical revolution. Each product had to be assembled from a given number of parts, any one of which could be replaced by an identical part. This method of manufacture was developed first in the production of guns in the early nineteenth century by Eli Whitney (1765–

1825), a New Englander who earlier had invented the cotton gin (1793) while studying law in Georgia. Others soon applied the principle of interchangeable parts to clocks, sewing machines, typewriters, and many other items. . . .

The rapid growth of the American economy depended also on an increasing specialization and division of labor. Relatively independent Jacks-of-all-trades (village blacksmiths, for example) gave way to many interdependent individuals skilled in particular economic activities. Most striking was the separation of labor and management functions, which arose slowly in agriculture but rapidly in industry. Specialized managers and specialized wage earners replaced semi-independent artisans; manual laborers no longer organized production or sold finished products. Specialized retailing replaced the general store; the jobber concentrated increasingly on a particular line of goods; investment bankers who floated stocks and bonds became separated from commercial bankers who made loans to business. The sole link among these specialists lay in the price-and-market system in which impersonal monetary values governed the relationships between buyers and sellers of labor, commodities, and credit. Those at the core of this price-and-market network, such as capitalists and business managers, possessed great power to manipulate it, while farmers and wage earners, far less capable of influencing large economic affairs, were more frequently manipulated by others. Thus, the closely knit economy of specialists gave rise to a division between dominant and subordinate, central and peripheral, economic roles.

A simpler distribution system, involving fewer middlemen and more direct buying and selling, replaced the innumerable traders formerly required. Previously manufacturers had sold almost exclusively to jobbers who stocked the goods of many different makers and forwarded them in turn to wholesalers. This system was defective for manufacturers: jobbers hesitated to push any particular line of goods, but manufacturers were eager to exploit the possibilities of a national market by rapidly expanding sales of their own goods. Manufacturers took over more and more of the process of distribution. In 1896, for example, the Pittsburgh Plate Glass Company, dissatisfied with the practices of its jobbers, established a chain of warehouses throughout the country to distribute its own products. Such firms, bypassing jobbers, sold directly to regional wholesalers and often to retailers as well as to industrial and institutional buyers. They developed active sales departments, spent increasing sums for advertising, and registered brand names at the Patent Office in order to distinguish their products from other standard, mass-produced items. Traveling salesmen now represented the producer, and

Rural Free Delivery (1896) and Parcel Post (1913) enabled manufacturers to sell to farmers without middlemen. Such innovations in mass retailing as the Sears-Roebuck and Montgomery Ward mail-order houses, the chains, and the department store, which often purchased directly from manufacturers, also contributed to a simpler and more efficient distribution system.

Changes in grain marketing dramatically illustrated the manner in which distribution became more efficient. Marketing facilities in Chicago, the new center of the grain trade, could not handle the immense amounts of wheat which railroads poured into the city from the Middle West in the 1850's and 1860's. A revolution in grain handling resulted. Wheat, formerly transported in bags and carried from railroad to lake vessel on human shoulders, now was shipped bulk in freight cars, dumped into endless chain-buckets, carried to the top of huge elevators, and dropped into ships. The savings in labor and the consequent decline in distribution costs were enormous. . . .

The tighter national and even international distribution network that linked grain producer and grain consumer symbolized the radical change which the transportation and communications revolution had created in agriculture. Formerly farmers had remained comparatively self-sufficient, producing much of their own food, clothing, furniture, and equipment. But just as the new national market destroyed the local blacksmith in the face of mass-produced hardware, no less did it outmode production by the farmer's wife in competition with the clothing manufacturer. Household industry remained longest in those areas which high-cost transportation rendered least accessible to the outside world and therefore where consumers were least able to purchase factory-made goods. The same revolution in transport, opening up new markets for the farmer, enabled him to earn more cash to purchase manufactured products. Subsistence farming, in other words, gave way to commercial farming. Instead of producing most of the items needed for his livelihood, the farmer became a specialist, concentrating on those crops that climate, soil, and ability enabled him to produce most profitably.

Technology contributed to this transformation. John Deere (1804–86), an Illinois blacksmith, began to produce a steel plow at Moline in 1847; it proved to be far superior to wooden and cast-iron plows in turning the tough virgin sods of the Middle West and rapidly reduced the cost of soil preparation. Even more spectacular were improvements in harvesting: the reaper, developed by Cyrus H. McCormick (1809–84) in the Middle West; the self-binder, which cut the grain and tied it into sheaves; and finally the huge combines, used on the broad wheat fields of the Red River

Valley of the North and of the Central Valley of California, which joined reaping and threshing in one operation powered by steam engines. Between 1830 and 1896 these new implements almost cut in half the time and labor cost of production for all crops; for wheat it reduced the time worked to one-twentieth that required for hand labor, and the labor cost to a fifth of the previous figure. But this machinery also increased the capital investment required for farming. Whereas in 1820 a farmer could buy adequate equipment for an average, well-managed family farm for $100, by 1900 a sum of $750 was needed, even though the price of farm machinery had declined sharply after 1880. Readily available capital funds became increasingly essential for agricultural enterprise and yet were frequently difficult to secure.

Cereal-growing farmers in the Middle and Far West adopted harvesting and threshing machinery during and soon after the Civil War. Southern and eastern crops, on the other hand, did not lend themselves to machine methods. The harvest of southern cotton and tobacco required careful hand labor, as did most operations in eastern truck, dairy, and fruit farming. The principal innovations in eastern agriculture consisted less in the use of machinery to replace manual operations and more in intensive scientific management: specialized dairy cattle breeding, insect and disease control, fertilizer, improved plant varieties, and new methods of preserving perishables. . . .

Markets, machinery, and science, then, transformed American agriculture from a relatively simple operation, requiring little capital and less knowledge, into a highly complex affair, demanding increasing amounts of investment, equipment, scientific information, and close attention to markets. The farmer was now irrevocably entwined in the complex industrial system. Not as a Jack-of-all-trades, but only as a calculating, alert, and informed businessman, could he survive.

Within this general pattern of economic change occurred considerable geographical specialization. Industry became concentrated north of the Ohio River and east of the Mississippi. Here were the new iron and steel mills, the textile and shoe factories, the lumber mills and furniture establishments, and hundreds of other firms; here was the densest railroad network in the country. A rich store of readily available resources, such as Pennsylvania coal, Middle Atlantic and Great Lakes lumber, and New England waterpower, partly determined this location of industry. In addition, the area's natural arteries provided the earliest and cheapest east-west transportation route. The Erie Canal, which penetrated the Appalachian chain at its lowest gap, linked the East with the Great Lakes. Railroads followed patterns that these earlier forms of transportation established. But the location of industry was influenced as well by the already existing concentration of commercial activity in the northeastern seaports of Boston, New York, Philadelphia, and Baltimore. Industry was attracted to these older urban centers because they were at the hub of growing transportation systems and because capital accumulated in commerce, as well as an adequate labor force, was more readily available there than elsewhere.

The South and the West, predominantly agricultural and mining areas, served as markets for northeastern products and as sources of its food and raw materials. Cotton, tobacco, and rice from the South, grain from the Middle West and the Pacific Coast, and beef from the Great Plains were carried to urban markets in the Northeast and in Europe. The primary processors of farm products migrated to these producing areas. As grain production shifted west from the Middle Atlantic states, so did flour milling—to St. Louis, then to Minneapolis and Kansas City. As beef and pork production moved to the western Middle West, the slaughtering capital of the nation shifted from Cincinnati to Chicago and finally to a half-dozen cities, such as Kansas City and Sioux City, on the edge of the cattle country. The West also shipped industrial raw materials eastward. Iron from the Lake Superior region, copper from the same area and later from Montana, Arizona, and Utah, lead and zinc from the Kansas-Missouri-Arkansas section, and lumber from the Pacific Northwest all contributed their share of the ingredients of northeastern industry. Little manufacturing developed in the West and the South save in a few specialized areas; those regions depended on the Northeast for their manufactured products, their clothing, hardware, farm machinery, and construction materials. Thus emerged a regional division of labor which the transportation network bound into a national economic system.

Within each geographical region, specialization between rural and urban areas grew rapidly. The city, the center of industrial activity, concentrated on producing manufactured goods, performing far more effectively functions that farmers had formerly undertaken. Rural areas, on the other hand, retained their specialty, food production. Cities served as the nerve centers of the new economy. To them came labor, capital, and raw materials; from them finished products were dispensed. They became great shipping points, manufacturing centers, and accumulations of capital, skill, and managerial ability. The core of the city was business, around which other human activities arose to fashion a social and cultural as well as an economic community. These industrial cities attracted millions of people from abroad and from the American countryside. The European newcomers arrived in waves that coincided roughly with the rise and fall of the nation's level of economic activity. An equally large number of people migrated from rural areas to the cities, especially in the industrial Northeast. Less prosperous farmers in that area, unable to meet western competition, sought their fortunes in the new urban centers. With the influx of population, industrial cities mushroomed beyond their original limits to become vast metropolitan centers.

PROBLEM 8

The Farmers

Following the passage of the Homestead Act of 1862, the building of railroads, and the arrival of millions of immigrants, farms sprang up west of the Mississippi. As you read in Problem 7, advances in technology in both agriculture and industry spurred this expansion. A succession of new and improved farm implements and methods enabled farmers to grow larger grain crops and to produce more beef and pork with less effort and less man power than ever before. The amount of food products increased faster than the growth of population, and as a result the prices of agricultural commodities fell.

To maintain incomes equal to their needs, many farmers added to the acreage they planted and purchased additional farm machinery to help increase crop yields.

This development produced larger crops than farmers were able to market profitably and brought further declines in prices. Farmers found themselves in a serious predicament.

If, for example, a man took out a mortgage for $4000 with which to buy a farm and machinery when wheat was selling for $1 a bushel, he might have planned to pay off most of his debt with 4000 bushels of wheat.

But if the price fell to fifty cents a bushel, he would have to raise and sell twice as many bushels to pay his mortgage.

If other farmers increased their crops for the same reason, prices undoubtedly fell still further. If a drought or a flood added to the farmer's difficulties, he probably had little or no extra cash to carry him through the emergency. Under these conditions, either a bad crop or a good one could mean disaster for him.

As overproduction of farm products grew steadily after the Civil War, many farmers ultimately faced ruin. But they did not blame overproduction for their plight. Instead they blamed the high fees charged for transportation by the railroads and singled out as enemies eastern industrialists, bankers, and businessmen who they suspected were growing rich at the farmers' expense.

To remedy their situation the farmers organized alliances such as the National Grange. Later they joined with other political groups to form the People's party, or the Populists. One of the main planks in their platform demanded the free and unlimited coinage of silver, a measure intended to induce inflation and to raise prices of agricultural products. Most of the Populists abandoned their party in 1896 to vote for the Democratic presidential candidate, William Jennings Bryan, who shared their views concerning the free coinage of silver. Bryan lost to William McKinley in two consecutive elections— in 1896 and in 1900—and free silver as a political issue grew less important as prices for agricultural products rose along with the general prosperity after 1900.

Problem 8 deals with some of these dramatic episodes in American agricultural history as it examines the position of the American farmer in the 1890's.

As you study the readings in this Problem, think about the following questions:

1 What kinds of problems troubled the farmers of the 1890's? How were they similar to those of the city workers? how different?

2 According to Shannon the farmer pictured himself as an individual capitalist. Could he cope with his problems as such? Does the Populist platform seem to reflect a capitalistic approach?

3 What did farmers blame for their troubles?

4 How were farm troubles related to the depression?

5 In times of depression as well as in prosperity, the percentage of the population engaged in farming steadily diminished. Do you find anything in the readings to account for this fact? What problems did the farmer have that could not be solved by general prosperity?

I

THE PLIGHT OF THE SOUTHERN FARMER

The following account tells of problems with which farmers contended in the 1890's. ☐ C. Vann Woodward, *The Origins of the New South,* pp. 269–270. Baton Rouge: Louisiana State University Press, copyright © 1951.

First and last, however, it was the farmers and the agricultural masses associated with them who suffered most bitterly in this depression. Conditions and prices that were bad enough in the eighties to provoke the angry protest of the Farmers' Alliance movement grew considerably worse in the nineties. "The outlook here is gloomier than since 1873 on account of crop failures and crop prices," wrote an Alabamian in the fall of 1892. Prices fell to less than half those of a decade earlier. The cotton farmers produced a crop in 1894 that exceeded by two million bales any crop previously grown; yet they received $50,000,000 less for it than for the crop of 1882. For people who depended upon cotton as their only source of cash income these prices meant destitution. The tobacco farmer's story was similar. The value placed upon the Virginia tobacco crop of 1894 was less than half the value of any crop since 1880 except 1888, and less than a third of the crop of 1881. The Kentucky crop of 1894 was valued at less than it had been since the seventies, and the 1895 crop went even lower. Of the 119 counties of Kentucky, 87 could not raise enough money in 1891 to pay the expenses of local government; schools as well as banks closed.

The lien system tightened its grip; mortgages increased and so did tenancy. The farmer fell more deeply into debt; and, as his debt increased, the money in which it was measured appreciated in terms of bales, and bushels, and pounds of his product. The Southern farmer listened with mounting anger to lectures upon his "financial integrity" from his Eastern creditors, who were enriched at his expense. "We have reached the stage where slow, reasoned arguments cannot any longer affect us," wrote a Kentuckian; "neither the ties of partisanship or political loyalty. It is a question of bread and meat, and we are ready to fight."

If Nature piled calamity upon the financial woes of the Western farmer, she was no kinder to the farmer of the South. Flood, drought, and plague competed with debt, mortgage, and bankruptcy as causes of suffering. Crevasses in the levees of the lower Mississippi in 1891, 1892, and 1893 resulted in floods that made thousands homeless and reduced many to the point of starvation. The floods drowned stock, destroyed property valued at several millions, and rendered much of the overflowed land unproductive for years.

Drought followed flood. Lack of water cut Louisiana rice production from 182,000,000 pounds in 1893 to 76,000,000 in 1895. Drought in 1896 caused an almost total loss of crops in the hill country of Louisiana, Mississippi, Arkansas, and Texas. The great freeze of 1894–1895 resulted in widespread suffering, and in Florida it brought disaster to the orange growers. Tropical storms lashed the sea islands and the Georgia coast in 1893, and the same year brought a recurrence of the yellow-fever epidemic on the Gulf Coast.

In 1892 a new and terrifying enemy began an invasion from Mexico that in future years was to overrun the cotton kingdom—the boll weevil.

II

TROUBLE ON THE PRAIRIES

Many of the first pioneers to establish free homestead claims on western lands in the 1860's settled in Nebraska, a Territory until 1867 when it became the 37th state of the Union. Population grew from about 2700 in 1854 to about 123,000 in 1870. In the 1880's another wave of homesteaders arrived, but drought and economic conditions drove many of them back East. In 1890 the state was afire with Populism; it was in Nebraska that the Populists held their first national convention. The following selection by a contemporary writer is an account of conditions among farmers in Nebraska during the 1890's. □ "The Destitution in Nebraska." New York: *Harper's Weekly,* Volume 39, January 19, 1895, pp. 59–62.

Unless the crop of 1895 is a remarkably bountiful one, a considerable share of the counties of western Nebraska will be nearly depopulated by next fall. As it is, two successive crop failures have sent thousands of families in search of more promising land and reduced thousands more to the verge of starvation.

In twelve or fourteen of the southwestern counties utter destitution exists, and unless generous supplies of food and fuel are promptly sent and systematically distributed, the most squalid of deaths will be the fate of many. There are hundreds of houses where the provision supplies do not exceed, all told, a pound a head. Scurvy, from insufficient food and the lack of vegetables, has made its appearance in some quarters, and physicians predict an epidemic of the disease unless a food remedy is quickly supplied. While the grazing is good, and some money is made by a few persons caring for herds of horses sent there for the winter from the eastern part of the State, feed will be needed in the early spring in order to put horses intended for field-work into condition for that labor. . . .

The great cattle companies, those gigantic stock combinations which we now hear of in Wyoming and Montana, once let their enormous herds roam over this section with little expense save herding. But the westward tide of farm immigration, enticed by the allurements of cheap land, soon drove the cattle to the west and north. The lands became more valuable for farm purposes than for grazing, and the herds finally fell back upon the Wyoming table-lands and foot-hills.

A great boom in Nebraska farm lands took place. Millions of dollars were invested by Eastern companies in the shape of loans made to the new men who took up this land and began breaking it up with the ploughshare. Some of it was magnificent land; better never was seen anywhere. There were few streams, to be sure, and whole counties without a tree or a shrub; but so long as rain fell and wells could be dug there seemed to be no need of streams, and as for trees, they could be planted. Many men took these acres up under the homestead law, but many others purchased outright, having sold property in Iowa, Illinois, and other States to the east. Men who held 80 or 160 acres in Illinois were dazzled with the discovery that by selling out they could purchase 320, or even 640, acres in western Nebraska for the price of their old land, and have enough money to move out with besides. Many and many were the instances where this was done. The temptation was alluring. The crops raised in Nebraska have been enormous. Corn often ran 100 bushels to the acre, and the work was done with infinitely less trouble and expense.

But gradually the climate, so far as rainfall is concerned, has changed, becoming drier every summer. Copious rains may fall in the planting season or in the fall, but when the growing season comes there is nothing to temper the heat or to refresh the crops in stalk. And the wind—it bloweth every day—and such a wind! Resistless, never-ceasing, dry and penetrating, hot as from the bowels of a volcano, a veritable furnace's breath, it sweeps these heights, these stretches of prairie and table-land, with the mercury at 90° and sometimes 100° Fahrenheit, for days at a time. A farmer in June may have two hundred acres of the finest corn that ever promised a crop—corn such as even Illinois cannot equal. He may go to bed in sight of this moving sea of green, and the next night may look out upon the total ruin of his fortune, so deadly to all vegetable life is the breath of this sirocco.

Since the middle of July, 1894, these farmers have been facing the most terrible situation human beings can be called by fate to look at. Again emigration started up. Prairie-schooners filled with farmers' families have made trails in all directions since then. Deserted sod houses line every road. You can drive in some parts for half a day and not see more than three or four inhabited dwellings. In many cases agricultural implements stand in the furrows just where they were left last summer. Often the houses are dismantled, but in many instances they are just as their owners left them.

But thousands still remain, either from inability to get away, or through a hope that in some way or other they may be enabled to exist through the winter and to put in the next year's crop. The Legislature will doubtless either advance money or loan it without interest for seed, but the maintenance of this population from now until next fall largely depends upon charity. In some few cases counties have small amounts of money at their disposal, by which the bare necessities of life may be obtained, but in the majority of cases fuel, food, and clothes are at this moment an urgent necessity for more than half the population.

III

FARM FACTS OF THE 1890'S

The following selection is written by a modern historian. In his analysis he compares the living standards of city worker and farmer during the 1890's. □ Fred A. Shannon, "The Status of the Midwestern Farmer in 1900." Lincoln, Nebraska: *Mississippi Valley Historical Review*, Volume 37, Number 3, December 1950, pp. 496–497, 503–504, 506–507.

If for the last century people had received what statisticians have generally rated as the cost of living, the main problems of society would have been solved long ago. It takes people who . . . learned by experience and close observation on what wage an average family could exist, and how much it took to make a comfortable living, to answer this question. On this basis of reckoning it can be asserted that the bulk of town and city industrial workers at unskilled tasks got in the neighborhood of $1.50 a day, or not more than $500 a year. On this wage the family of the laborer lived, but only by desperate skimping. Rent at above $6.00 a month was prohibitive, and dwellings at less than that sum were abominable. Only one stove at a time could be kept hot—the front-room stove or the cookstove—and there could be no heat at all at night. Blocks of wood roasted in the oven while supper was being cooked could be put in the beds to keep feet warm, but icicles on the covers where the breath played all night were the usual first view on awakening. . . . A pound of beefsteak at a cost of 15 cents might be had most any Sunday, and when the family wanted to gorge themselves on meat they could buy three pounds of liver for the same price, . . . [provided], of course, that they could convince themselves that liver was meat. For the rest of the week there was a long monotony of "sowbosom" and beans. The family getting $1,000 a year could have no real luxuries, but they could keep warm and the children could have overcoats and an extra pair of shoes. They could even afford to go on an occasional trolley car excursion.

These figures—$500 a year for existence and $1,000 for decent comfort—can also be used for the farm family, considering the value of food raised and consumed and the rental value of the farm home as a part of the income. . . .

. . . [It] is obvious that few farms of under 100 acres paid more than bare subsistence and that for most of them there had to be some supplementary source even for a drab existence. Though the tracts of from 50 to 100 acres appear at first glance to be slightly over the subsistence hump, a deduction of only $20 for expenses other than labor and fertilizer would put them below it. . . . But some 200,626 tenants and managers in the next size classification (100–175 acres) belonged to the submarginal horde, thus increasing the total to 57 per cent of all operators. Farm owners and tenants with over 260 acres may, in general, be classed as netting somewhere around $1,000 or more a year, with the exception of a number of tenants and managers too small to make any substantial difference in the general estimate. But operators below that level numbered 88.8 per cent of them all. . . .

. . . Add the number of submarginal farm operators to the number of hired men[1] and 2,624,000 out of all 3,625,000 farm-income receivers are accounted for, or 72.4 per cent making less than subsistence. Add the operators making less than $1,000 a year to the hired hands, and 91.6 per cent are found to be making less than a modest competence. Out of each thousand, 276 were making both ends meet and 84 of these were getting along comfortably or were prospering. This may help to explain why the old song, "Stay on the Farm," gained few converts; why the drift of population was from the country to the town; why so many sons of the soil had no love for the agricultural ladder, down which they had climbed from ownership to tenancy, from tenancy to hired labor, and from which they had fled to the city. . . .

. . . The present study shows that with all the Midwest's superiority in output, few producers made in excess of a scant living. Money was amassed

[1]Three eighths of all receivers of farm income were farm laborers.—*John Sperling*.

by holders of large areas farmed by tenants, and by other absentee landlords; money was gathered in by the creditors; some money was made beyond the needs for a comfortable living by about one person in twelve engaged in agricultural occupations.

Yet, farmers were coming to think of theirs as a capitalistic business, and so it was. The rule for such a business is that a few prosper and the rest exist. A few lay down the rules, stack the cards and deal them, and the rest play the game, hoping, like Wilkins Micawber [in *David Copperfield*], that something will turn up for them too. The backbone of the support of the Populist movement was made up of persons struggling to put farming on a par with other capitalistic businesses. They were about as radical as the smaller manufacturing capitalists who in the same period were trying to avoid being swallowed up by the big monopolies.

IV

THE SOLUTION AS THE FARMER SAW IT

The Populist party, named the People's Party of the U.S.A., was organized in February 1892 and held its first national convention in Omaha, Nebraska, in July. Delegates to the convention wrote a platform by which they hoped to solve a variety of problems—including the difficulties of the farmers—if their candidates for President and Vice-President were elected. The following selection is from the Populist platform. ☐ Edward McPherson, *A Handbook of Politics for 1892*, pp. 269–270. Washington, D.C.: James J. Chapman, copyright © 1892.

The conditions which surround us best justify our co-operation; we meet in the midst of a nation brought to the verge of moral, political, and material ruin. Corruption dominates the ballot box, the Legislatures, the Congress, and touches even the ermine of the Bench. The people are demoralized; most of the States have been compelled to isolate the voters at the polling places to prevent universal intimidation or bribery. The newspapers are largely subsidized or muzzled, public opinion silenced, business prostrated, our homes covered with mortgages, labor impoverished, and the land concentrating in the hands of capitalists. The urban workmen are denied the right of organization for self-protection, imported pauperized labor beats down their wages, a hireling standing army, unrecognized by our laws, is established to shoot them down, and they are rapidly degenerating into European conditions. The fruits of the toil of millions are boldly stolen to build up colossal fortunes for a few, unprecedented in the history of mankind, and the possessors of these in turn despise the Republic and endanger liberty. From the same prolific womb of governmental injustice we breed the two great classes—tramps and millionaires.

The national power to create money is appropriated to enrich bond-holders; a vast public debt, payable in legal tender currency, has been funded into gold-bearing bonds, thereby adding millions to the burdens of the people.

Silver, which has been accepted as coin since the dawn of history, has been demonetized to add to the purchasing power of gold by decreasing the value of all forms of property as well as human labor, and the supply of currency is purposely abridged to fatten usurers, bankrupt enterprise and enslave industry.

A vast conspiracy against mankind has been organized on two continents, and it is rapidly taking possession of the world. If not met and overthrown at once it forebodes terrible social convulsions, the destruction of civilization, or the establishment of an absolute despotism. . . .

FARMERS' DEMANDS

Our country finds itself confronted by conditions for which there is no precedent in the history of the world; our annual agricultural productions amount to billions of dollars in value, which must within a few weeks or months be exchanged for billions of dollars' worth of commodities consumed in their production; the existing currency supply is wholly inadequate to make the exchange; the results are falling prices, the formation of combines and rings, the impoverishment of the producing class.

We pledge ourselves that, if given power, we will labor to correct these evils by wise and reasonable legislation, in accordance with the terms of our platform.

We believe that the powers of government—in other words, of the people—should be expanded (as in the case of the postal service) as rapidly and as far as the good sense of an intelligent people and the teachings of experience shall justify, to the end that oppression, injustice and poverty, shall eventually cease in the land. . . .

. . . We declare, therefore—

PERPETUAL LABOR UNION

First—that the union of the labor forces of the United States this day consummated shall be permanent and perpetual; may its spirit enter into all hearts for the salvation of the Republic and the uplifting of mankind.

WEALTH FOR WORKERS

Second—Wealth belongs to him who creates it, and every dollar taken from industry without an equivalent is robbery. "If any will not work, neither shall he eat." The interests of rural and civic labor are the same; their enemies are identical.

OWNERSHIP OF RAILWAYS

Third—We believe that the time has come when the railroad corporations will either own the people or the people must own the railroads; and should the Government enter upon the work of owning and managing all railroads, we should favor an amendment to the Constitution by which all persons engaged in the Government service shall be placed under a civil service regulation of the most rigid character, so as to prevent the increase of the power of the national administration by the use of such additional Government employes.

FINANCE

1st.   We demand a national currency, safe, sound and flexible, issued by the General Government only, a full legal tender for all debts, public and private, and that without the use of banking corporations; a just, equitable and efficient means of distribution direct to the people at a tax not to exceed 2 per cent, per annum, to be provided as set forth in the Sub-Treasury plan of the Farmers' Alliance, or a better system; also be payments in discharge of its obligations for public improvements.

(A) We demand free and unlimited coinage of silver and gold at the present legal ratio of 16 to 1 [that is, 16 ounces of silver equal to 1 ounce of gold].

(B) We demand that the amount of circulating medium be speedily increased to not less than $50 per capita.

(C) We demand a graduated income tax.

(D) We believe that the money of the country should be kept as much as possible in the hands of the people, and hence we demand that all State and National revenues shall be limited to the necessary expenses of the Government, economically and honestly administered.

(E) We demand that Postal Savings Banks be established by the Government for the safe deposit of the earnings of the people and to facilitate exchange.

TRANSPORTATION

2nd.   Transportation being a means of exchange and a public necessity, the government should own and operate the railroads in the interest of the people. The telegraph and telephone, like the post office system, being a necessity for the transmission of news, should be owned and operated by the Government in the interest of the people.

LAND

3d. The land, including all the natural sources of wealth, is the heritage of the people and should not be monopolized for speculative purposes, and alien ownership of land should be prohibited. All land now held by railroads and other corporations in excess of their actual needs, and all lands now owned by aliens should be reclaimed by the Government and held for actual settlers only.

PROBLEM 9

Government Response to the Depression

The federal government had done little to lessen suffering caused by the depression which struck the nation in the wake of the Panic of 1837. In the course of time, prosperity returned and men forgot the dark days of the early 1840's. Several other depressions hit the nation during the nineteenth century, particularly in the 1850's and 1870's, but each time the government avoided direct assistance.

On the whole during the nineteenth century men looked upon government spending as they did on family budgets. If a wage-earner became unemployed, the family reduced expenditures. Similarly, if a depression hit the country, many persons reasoned that the federal government should reduce spending to compensate for the loss of income which accompanied a business recession. Consequently, no relief was provided nor were work projects created for the unemployed.

It had always been the responsibility of government to keep the peace and to protect property, however. As a depression deepened, many riots broke out. Hungry people fought to get food; farmers rose up against authorities to stop sheriffs from selling their farms; and workers organized strikes to win a raise in pay or to resist a wage reduction. When such incidents occurred, federal and local officials were usually quick to take action against the rebellious groups. Instead of getting at the source of the trouble by making jobs or offering relief to the unemployed, governments often called out the troops to drive strikers off the streets.

Troubles that were national in scope were left to whatever solution state and municipal governments could work out. But many states and cities also took a hands-off attitude. In New York, for example, thousands were unemployed in 1894. Governor Roswell P. Flower, however, vetoed the public works program proposed by the legislature, expressing the sentiment of one of President Grover Cleveland's famous statements: "In America, the people support the government; it is not the province of the government to support the people."

Other states, mainly in the West, tried with little success to meet the needs of their citizens. Widespread strikes and bloody labor violence furnished eloquent testimony that the troubles could not be solved solely on the local level. Whenever government officials would not or could not provide relief, the unemployed fell back upon the charitable instincts of the American people, but help from private sources was far from adequate.

As you read the four accounts in Problem 9 of the role of government in the depression of the 1890's, think about the following questions:

1 On what grounds did President Cleveland veto the bill to send seed to farmers? What conception of the role of government does the veto imply?

2 What is to be inferred from the President's reception of Coxey's army about his idea of the function of government in a depression?

3 Did Pingree's "solution" to unemployment look forward to increasing industrialization or did it hark back to the agrarian past of America? Was his program aimed at the depression?

4 Did President McKinley's philosophy differ from that of Cleveland or of Pingree?

I

COLD COMFORT TO THE FARMER

During Grover Cleveland's first administration, from 1885 to 1889, a drought struck Texas. Congress passed a modest bill authorizing the Commissioner of Agriculture to distribute seed grains to farmers. Cleveland's veto message to the House of Representatives in 1887 illustrates the attitude he later took in regard to government intervention in the depression of the 1890's. ☐ George F. Parker, Editor, *The Writings and Speeches of Grover Cleveland*, pp. 449–451. New York: Cassell Publishing Company, copyright © 1892.

EXECUTIVE MANSION
WASHINGTON, February 16, 1887.

TO THE HOUSE OF REPRESENTATIVES:

I return without my approval House bill number ten thousand two hundred and three, entitled "An Act to enable the Commissioner of Agriculture to make a special distribution of seeds in drought-stricken counties of Texas, and making an appropriation therefor."

It is represented that a long-continued and extensive drought has existed in certain portions of the State of Texas, resulting in a failure of crops and consequent distress and destitution.

Though there has been some difference in statements concerning the extent of the people's needs in the localities thus affected, there seems to be no doubt that there has existed a condition calling for relief; and I am willing to believe that, notwithstanding the aid already furnished, a donation of seed-grain to the farmers located in this region, to enable them to put in new crops, would serve to avert a continuance or return of an unfortunate blight.

And yet I feel obliged to withhold my approval of the plan as proposed by this bill, to indulge a benevolent and charitable sentiment through the appropriation of public funds for that purpose.

I can find no warrant for such an appropriation in the Constitution, and I do not believe that the power and duty of the general government ought to be extended to the relief of individual suffering which is in no manner properly related to the public service or benefit. A prevalent tendency to disregard the limited mission of this power and duty should, I think, be steadfastly resisted to the end that the lesson should be constantly enforced that, though the people support the government, the government should not support the people.

The friendliness and charity of our countrymen can always be relied upon to relieve their fellow-citizens in misfortune. This has been repeatedly and quite lately demonstrated. Federal aid in such cases encourages the expectation of paternal care on the part of the government and weakens the sturdiness of our national character, while it prevents the indulgence among our people of that kindly sentiment and conduct which strengthen the bonds of a common brotherhood.

It is within my personal knowledge that individual aid has, to some extent, already been extended to the sufferers mentioned in this bill. The failure of the proposed appropriation of ten thousand dollars additional, to meet their remaining wants, will not necessarily result in continued distress if the emergency is fully made known to the people of the country.

It is here suggested that the Commissioner of Agriculture is annually directed to expend a large sum of money for the purchase, propagation, and distribution of seeds and other things of this description, two-thirds of which are, upon the request of senators, representatives, and delegates in Congress, supplied to them for distribution among their constituents.

The appropriation of the current year for this purpose is one hundred thousand dollars, and it will probably be no less in the appropriation for the ensuing year. I understand that a large quantity of grain is furnished for such distribution, and it is supposed that this free apportionment among their neighbors is a privilege which may be waived by our senators and representatives.

If sufficient of them should request the Commissioner of Agriculture to send their shares of the grain thus allowed them, to the suffering farmers of Texas, they might be enabled to sow their crops; the constituents, for whom in theory this grain is intended, could well bear the temporary deprivation, and the donors would experience the satisfaction attending deeds of charity.

GROVER CLEVELAND

II

THE PRESIDENT RECEIVES COXEY'S ARMY

As unemployment worsened during 1894, bands composed mainly of hard-working and serious men began to march on Washington to demand relief. They won the sympathy of people in the towns through which they passed. The most famous band was an army led by an Ohio businessman named Jacob S. Coxey. He and about five hundred volunteers descended on the capital to demand that President Cleveland put unemployed men to work on useful internal improvements. When the army arrived, the President ordered that the marchers be stopped and he called out the entire city police force and a body of federal troops to halt them.

Thousands of people had gathered along Pennsylvania Avenue and near the Capitol to greet Coxey's army.

A reporter for one current publication, the *Outlook,* noted that of greater significance than "the five hundred recruits who made up the Coxey army" was "the sympathy shown them by the greater part of the fifteen or twenty thousand people who crowded the streets and lined the walks and terraces of Capitol Hill."

After the episode described in this reading, Coxey and his two major lieutenants, Carl Browne and Christopher Jones, were arrested for walking on the grass. They were sentenced to twenty days in jail and ordered to pay a five-dollar fine. ☐ From *Coxey's Army* by Donald L. McMurry, pp. 116–118. By permission of Little, Brown and Company, Boston. Copyright © 1929 by Donald L. McMurry.

Up the Avenue the Commonweal [Army] marched, amidst cheers, toward the Capitol. But barring the way, at the end of the Avenue, a solid phalanx of police extended from curb to curb. The decisive moment had arrived. The army turned aside, as if to march by, and then halted on B Street. Coxey, Browne, and Jones, after a hurried conference, walked alone toward the Capitol. They were discovered and the mounted police galloped after them. The three Commonweal leaders went over the low stone paling that surrounded the grounds and disappeared in the shrubbery; the police jumped their horses over and followed, and the crowd surged after them. Browne, conspicuous in his buckskins and sombrero, had almost reached the foot of the steps when two policemen threw themselves upon him. "I am an American citizen," he shouted, "I stand on my constitutional rights." He was handled roughly and hustled away. Coxey succeeded in reaching the steps, where he was recognized and surrounded. He asked to be allowed to speak, but that was forbidden. He then drew from his pocket a written protest which he had prepared for this contingency, but he was led away without being permitted to read it. As he passed a group of reporters he tossed his protest toward them, saying, "That is for the press." Jones was also taken into custody. The crowd about the foot of the steps shouted angrily. As Coxey, who had been thrust through the dense mass of humanity by the police climbed into the carriage where Mrs. Coxey with [their son] little Legal Tender awaited him, a "fierce cheer went up," and the police, who seem to have lost their heads completely, began to use their clubs; the mounted police charged, and fifty or more people were beaten or trampled.

During all this excitement the army had stood passively in line where its leaders had left it. It was led back to the camp by Jesse Coxey and his sister, "followed by hundreds of poorly dressed men and women, who cheered it all the way without intermission." Although Coxey was released by the officers after he had been led away from the Capitol steps, Browne and Jones were taken to jail, but they were soon bailed out. That evening Browne, considerably battered, returned to camp, made a speech, and issued "Special Order Number I", in which, with references to the Rothschilds, Belshazzar of old, good roads, and the "damp, dark dungeon" in which he had been confined for nearly five hours, he announced:

"Liberty lies weltering in her own blood in the Nation's Capital City to-night, stabbed in the home of friends and supposed guardians. Free speech has been suppressed and police clubs have taken the place of the scales of justice. . . . Brothers, we have entered upon the beginning of the end."

III

LOCAL GOVERNMENT AND THE DEPRESSION

Hazen Pingree, mayor of Detroit, developed a project which provided relief for some of the most needy people in his city. His plan, involving about 945 families, is described in the following excerpt. In 1894 Detroit had about 25,000 unemployed persons, about a tenth of the total population, and except for Pingree's project, nothing was done for the needy. □ H. P. Pingree, "Mayor Pingree's Potato Patch Plan." New York: *Public Opinion*, Volume 20, January 23, 1896, p. 109; February 13, 1896, pp. 205–206.

The plan of utilizing the vacant lands in the suburbs of the city was first conceived by me when the hard times of 1894 compelled so many people to be without employment. They were standing idly about the city, and as a large majority of the working element of every city come from the country, and are accustomed to and skilled in tilling the soil, I believed that with such a vast amount of vacant and unused land as surrounds the city of Detroit, there was a good opportunity to put these men in a way of securing a subsistence for the ensuing winter, by giving them a chance to cultivate it. I requested the use of it, and within a remarkably short time more land was placed at our disposal than could be used on account of the lateness of the season and the fact that no provision had been made for raising money to defray expenses for plowing and purchasing seeds. . . . Applicants were given a piece of land to cultivate according to their needs. About 3,000 applications were made for lots, but owing to lack of funds, the committee was able to provide for only 945 families. All applicants were carefully investigated, and none but worthy persons with families were helped. Seed potatoes, beans, and other seeds were furnished by the committee to those unable to provide them, the entire expenses of the committee being $3,600. . . .

The committee estimates that the potato crop averaged about 15 bushels per lot, which would give 14,175 bushels of potatoes alone. Large quantities of beans, turnips, and other vegetables were raised and daily consumed, of which the committee is unable to furnish a record. The estimated total value of the crops produced was \$12,000 to \$14,000, at a cost to the committee of about \$3,600. This latter sum was made up by subscriptions, and the difficulty the committee had in obtaining it was a matter of astonishment to me. Over one-half the amount was contributed by city employees. Although the plan itself was based upon the soundest common sense, it was treated by some with indifference, by others with ridicule, and by many as a huge joke. . . .

But the unqualified success of the experiment has silenced the croakers. Poor people almost fought for a chance to get a patch of ground to till, and those who were successful used their best efforts to obtain a full crop. Applications for land for 1895 were made by a large proportion of them. The loss by theft was practically nothing, certainly not more than that of the average market gardener. In giving out the ground, politics was not considered. . . .

It seems to me the experiment has clearly demonstrated:

(1) That at least 95 per cent of the people who are in destitute circumstances, as a result of the hard times, are ready, willing, and anxious to work.

(2) That a large number of these people can be supported by utilizing vacant land in the outskirts of the city.

(3) That a very small space of ground is sufficient to raise enough vegetables to support a family through the winter.

(4) That a majority of our citizens who own vacant land would much rather allow it to be cultivated by the poor than to pay a large tax for their support.

(5) That the needy are thereby assisted without creating the demoralization in the habit of the people that gratuitous aid always entails. . . .

The educational part of the plan is really worth more than the thousands of dollars of benefit received in the crops. Every one will concede that we have drifted from nature's own way of getting a livelihood. Rushing to the cities and trying to get a livelihood by one's wits is not nature's way, and this agricultural plan will be, I believe, a step in the right direction. . . . From the results of this plan, I am satisfied that large cities will do well to set apart certain sections of land for permanent use in this direction. This will become more and more apparent as the large cities become more and more populous, and no man can do a more philanthropic act than to donate land for such use. I would even favor the municipalities purchasing land for this purpose. . . .

To conclude, I would say that for the benefit of the health of those who live in crowded cities; for the education it affords, as to the natural way to earn an honest living, and for the direct good to the poor themselves, as well as for the use of matter that is now wasted, I can conceive of no other plan that will do as much good.

IV

PRESIDENT McKINLEY ADVISES HIS FELLOW CITIZENS

In his inaugural address on March 4, 1897, President McKinley counseled his countrymen on how best to meet the challenges of chronic unemployment, business failure, social unrest, and violence. ☐ William McKinley, *The Speeches and Addresses of William McKinley*, pp. 7–9, 13–14. New York: Doubleday & McClure Company, copyright © 1900.

The depression of the past four years has fallen with especial severity upon the great body of toilers of the country, and upon none more than the holders of small farms. Agriculture has languished and labor suffered. The revival of manufacturing will be a relief to both. No portion of our population is more devoted to the institutions of free government, nor more loyal in their support, while none bears more cheerfully or fully its proper share in the maintenance of the government, or is better entitled to its wise and liberal care and protection. Legislation helpful to producers is beneficial to all. The depressed condition of industry on the farm and in the mine and factory has lessened the ability of the people to meet the demands upon them; and .they rightfully expect that not only a system of revenue shall be established that will secure the largest income with the least burden, but that every means will be taken to decrease, rather than increase, our public expenditures. Business conditions are not the most promising. It will take time to restore the prosperity of former years. If we cannot promptly attain it, we can resolutely turn our faces in that direction and aid its return by friendly legislation. However troublesome the situation may appear, Congress will not, I am sure, be found lacking in disposition or ability to relieve it as far as legislation can do so. The restoration of confidence and the revival of business, which men of all parties so much desire, depend more largely upon the prompt, energetic, and intelligent action of Congress than upon any other single agency affecting the situation. . . .

It has been the uniform practice of each President to avoid, as far as possible, the convening of Congress in extraordinary session. It is an example which, under ordinary circumstances and in the absence of a public necessity, is to be commended. But a failure to convene the representatives of the people in Congress in extra session when it involves neglect of a public duty places the responsibility of such neglect upon the Executive himself. The condition of the public Treasury, as has been indicated, demands the immediate consideration of Congress. It alone has the power to provide revenues for the government. Not to convene it under such circumstances I can view in no other sense than the neglect of a plain duty. I do not sympathize with the sentiment that Congress in session is dangerous to our general business interests. Its members are the agents of the people, and their presence at the seat of government in the execution of the sovereign will should not operate as an injury, but a benefit. There could be no better time to put the government upon a sound financial and economic basis than now. The people have only recently voted that this should be done, and nothing is more binding upon the agents of their will than the obligation of immediate action.

The Depression of 1893–1898:
An Interpretation

Although the depression of 1893–1898 was not so severe nor so prolonged as that of the 1840's, it was probably the worst of the early industrial depressions. The social and political conflicts it developed were more dramatic than those of the days of Andrew Jackson. The origins, progress, and results of the depression of 1893–1898 illustrate vividly the changes which fifty years wrought in the nature of American society. In an economic sense the years from 1837 to 1844 marked the end of the eighteenth century; those from 1893 to 1898 ushered in the twentieth.

Up to the 1840's America was an agricultural-commercial nation with only a little manufacturing. The ebb and flow of its economic life was governed by the seasons, the weather, the movement of peoples, and the gyrations of politics. Long-term economic growth was slow; real annual income per capita rose at approximately one half of 1 per cent for the first forty years of the nineteenth century, a rate similar to that of the pre-industrial economy of the eighteenth century. The increasing pace of industrialization after 1840 brought a dramatic increase in the rate of economic development. The average annual growth in real income per capita rose threefold, to about 1¾ per cent.

As the economy grew, industry played an increasing role in the rise and fall of the economy. The fluctuations in the rate of economic growth took on an apparent cyclical pattern, that is, there seemed to be periodic cycles during which economic activity would rise to a peak of prosperity, slip into a depression, and then begin another rise. Economists are not certain about the causes, duration, or timing of these cycles, and some believe that economic fluctuation might not have a cyclical pattern at all.

Generally, however, economists identify two cycles of different lengths, the long swing and the business cycle. The long swing lasts from ten to twenty years, and the short cycle, or business cycle, from two to five years. The long swings are marked by surges of economic growth during which there are sustained increases in the size of population, the investment of capital, and general economic activity. These surges are followed by a decline in which all of these factors grow at a much slower rate. During the surges, the rate of growth in the output of the economy is two or three times as great as during the declines. The causes of these long swings have yet to be isolated, but changes in the rate of the growth of population have been tentatively identified as the force which sets them in motion.

The business cycle, or short cycle, is produced by an imbalance in the way an economy grows. Let us start, for example, when business activity and the prices of materials, labor, and capital are low. First, production will begin to rise as consumers and business firms respond to the opportunities offered by low prices. The rise in production will continue as long as materials, labor, and capital are available at low enough prices to insure profits. Second, business firms will make plans for increased future production which cannot be developed without causing a rise in the prices of materials, labor, and capital. As these plans are carried out, prices rise and profits begin to fall because consumers will not buy so much at higher prices. Third, in the face of falling profits, business firms cut back production, bringing a loss of income to workers. These workers are also consumers. Hence, consumer demand begins to fall and business firms cut production even more. Fourth, as production and consumption fall, the demand for materials, labor, and capital falls and prices decline. This decline continues until prices fall far enough to make increased production profitable again. Then the cycle begins anew.

The long swings and the business cycles are closely related. The long swing movements help to increase the level of prosperity during the upward movement of a business cycle and to lower the depth of depression when the business cycle turns down. When the long swing is moving upward, periods of prosperity are strong and depressions are mild and brief. When the long swing is going down, the opposite happens. Periods of prosperity are short and of modest proportions, and depressions are deep and long lasting. Between the Civil War and the beginning of World War II, the bottom point of the long swings always ended in a severe and prolonged depression. Recovery from these depressions did not occur until the long swing started into a new upward phase. The depression that began in 1893 was one of these periods at the bottom of a long swing.

The reading in Problem 10, although it omits discussion of the business cycle, is an interpretation of the causes of the depression of the 1890's. As you read it, think about the following questions:

1 What have been the major interpretations of the causes of the depression in the 1890's?

2 What is Faulkner's interpretation?

3 What light does this reading shed on the importance of the federal government in fighting depressions? on the importance of the President?

THE DEPRESSION EXPLAINED

Harold Underwood Faulkner, a noted American economic historian, discusses some ways in which people in the past interpreted the depression of the 1890's. Faulkner also gives his own interpretation of this dramatic period of American history. □ Harold Underwood Faulkner, *Politics, Reform and Expansion, 1890–1900*, pp. 141–147, 161–162. New York: Harper & Row, Publishers. Copyright © 1959 by Harold Underwood Faulkner.

"There has never been a time in our history," said Benjamin Harrison in his last message to Congress, "when work was so abundant, or when wages were as high, whether measured by the currency in which they are paid, or by their power to supply the necessaries and comforts of life." Within months the worst financial panic in years broke over the country. Ten days before Harrison left office [in March 1893] the Philadelphia and Reading Railroad, with no warning, suddenly went bankrupt. The volume of sales on the day of its collapse was the greatest in the history of the New York Stock Exchange. The air was filled with anxiety. The unfortunate Cleveland was installed in the White House. Then on May 5 the National Cordage Company failed in spectacular fashion, shortly after paying its regular dividend. The market collapsed abruptly. Banks called in their loans; the stream of credit dried to a trickle. Businesses failed daily. The Erie went down in July, the Northern Pacific in August, the Union Pacific in October, the Atchison in December.

Before the year was out, 500 banks and nearly 16,000 businesses had declared themselves bankrupt.

"The month of August" [wrote the *Commercial and Financial Chronicle*] "will long remain memorable . . . in our industrial history. Never before has there been such a sudden and striking cessation of industrial activity. Nor was any section of the country exempt from the paralysis. Mills, factories, furnaces, mines nearly everywhere shut down in large numbers, and commerce and enterprise were arrested in an extraordinary degree . . . and hundreds of thousands of men thrown out of employment."

By September, according to the *Banker's Magazine* of London, the American people were "in the throes of a fiasco unprecedented even in their broad experience." "Ruin and disaster run riot over the land."

The panic broadened into a major depression. In the following year railroad traffic for the second time in history suffered an absolute decline. Railroad construction fell off drastically, reaching its lowest point since 1851. By 1895, new mileage shrank to 1,800 as compared to 4,700 in 1892. By the end of June, 1894, more than 40,818 miles and one-fourth of the capitalization of American railroads were in the hands of receivers. Three-fifths of railroad stock paid no dividends. Investment in all businesses declined sharply; new stock issues on the New York Exchange dropped from $100 million in 1892 to less than $37 million in 1894. Consumption of consumer goods fell in 1894 to 75 per cent of capacity, and wages and prices tumbled after consumption, both dropping at least 10 per cent. Unemployment mounted alarmingly, although in the absence of accurate statistics it was difficult to know exactly how many workers were out of a job at any given time. *Bradstreet's* estimated the unemployed in August, 1893, as about 850,000, but Richard T. Ely put the figure at 2 million. Gompers in December put it at 3 million. During the worst months of 1894 it is safe to conclude that as much as 20 per cent of the labor force was unemployed. In New York the police at one time estimated that 67,280 were out of work and 20,000 more were not only out of work but homeless and vagrant. In Chicago, more than 100,000 were jobless during the winter of 1893–94.

The year 1895 brought a brief improvement, but in 1896 a second shock caused a further decline, and economic activity plunged to 75 per cent of capacity in 1897. By that time the number of bank failures since 1893 had reached 800. "Men died like flies under the strain," wrote Henry Adams, "and Boston grew suddenly old, haggard and thin." Stock prices reached their lowest point in August, 1896, when they stood at 68 per cent of the level of August, 1892. Not until 1898 did recovery begin to be apparent; in that year the drain of gold from the country, continuous since 1889, finally ceased, and consumption of perishable goods regained its 1892 level. Not until 1901 or 1902 could the country be said to have been functioning normally, and even then many areas still suffered from the lingering effects of the depression.

There was no agreement as to the causes of the depression; one's explanation depended on one's political predilections. Conservatives agreed with Cleveland in attributing it to the Sherman Silver Purchase Act [passed in 1890 by Congress, requiring the federal government to purchase 4½ million ounces of silver each month and to issue paper money against it], which they believed had undermined business confidence in the gold standard. Beyond this, they blamed radical attacks on property. E. L. Godkin of *The Nation,* William Graham Sumner of Yale, and J. Lawrence Laughlin of Chicago University elaborated this view at great length. Godkin believed that the depression was the work of "socialists and labor agitators" who had been "filling the bellies of the poor with the east wind." "The craze against property that has been sweeping through the country," he said, sapped the national morale; what the country needed was respect for property, character, and authority. For Laughlin, the depression was "the inevitable manifestation of an idea strongly held by under-educated men."

Labor leaders and agrarians took a very different view of the matter. Samuel Gompers laid the depression to capitalistic greed. For years, he said, "Production, production, production, faster, greater, was the impulse, the thought, and motive of the capitalist class," even as the rights of the laboring man were being forgotten. The moral was clear: if labor's demands had been heeded, "it is safe to say that the panic of 1893 would have been averted, deferred, and certainly less intense." The agrarian radicals likewise blamed the depression on the capitalists, but they emphasized the money issue, arguing that it was the failure to introduce free silver coinage that had caused the crisis. It was left to Henry Adams, however, to carry the theme of conspiracy to its extreme; the panic, he wrote, was the result of a "dark, mysterious, crafty, rapacious, and tyrannical power . . . to rob and oppress and enslave the people."

These were by no means the only explanations offered; everybody had his own interpretation of what had happened, in which his particular enemies were exclusively to blame. The Democrats blamed the depression on the Republicans, noting that Republican laws were still in effect when the panic began. The Republicans accused the Democrats of having frightened the business community with their reckless talk of lowering the tariff. Only a few contemporary commentators penetrated the fog of political prejudice to show that the events of 1893 were part of a longer development and that no single party or program could be held responsible for a failure in which the whole country was directly or indirectly involved.

In retrospect it is possible to distinguish a number of deeper causes of the depression. In the first place, many industries, in particular the railroads, had expanded their activities far beyond the market demand. During the 1880's almost 74,000 miles of railroad were built, more than during any previous decade. Much of this expansion was dictated not by any reasonable estimate of traffic possibilities but by the pressure of competition; each road recklessly and hastily threw up lines that were not needed, through miles and miles of uninhabited wilderness, merely to insure that another road would not claim the territory first. Inevitably enterprises built on dreams and credit had to collapse; when the dreams failed to materialize, credit also evaporated. The fortunes of other industries, like steel, were bound up with those of the railroads, and when the railroads began to fail one by one in the summer of 1893, the failure quickly spread to other sectors of the economy; thirty-two steel corporations failed during the first six months of 1893. Economic activitiy in the United States had reached a new stage of interdependence, and a weakness in the very heart of the system unavoidably enfeebled the rest. The same conditions characterized banking. Formerly failures in one part of the country had not necessarily caused failures in other parts. By 1890, however, banking had become centralized in New York, where a large proportion of the country's reserve capital inexorably gravitated. Moreover, these reserves had been freely used in speculation. When stocks fell, many city banks fell with them; and since the city banks held up to 60 per cent of the reserves of other banks throughout the country, the panic, once it had seized New York, almost immediately became nationwide.

. . . [The] depression . . . of 1893 was preceded by several years of agricultural depression. In 1880 agriculture produced 26 per cent of the national wealth; in 1890 it produced only 21 per cent. Such a decline in the value of agricultural commodities represented a considerable decline in purchasing power which was not made up elsewhere—what was lost in agriculture was made up in the expansion of industries which were already overexpanded. The farmer's real income had declined steadily . . . since 1888. When he pleaded for relief, he was told, in effect, that his troubles were no concern of the rest of the nation. The prolonged depression of the nineties gave the lie to that opinion. The fact was that agriculture, like practically everything else, had expanded rapidly in the 1880's, compelling expansion in many other industries as well. The railroads, the manufacture of farm machinery, and many other businesses thrived on the expansion of agriculture and could hardly help to escape eventual involvement in its decline.

Without these existing weaknesses in the American economy, it would not have been so vulnerable to blows which it began to receive from abroad. In 1890 the failure of Baring Brothers [a banking firm] in London resulted in considerable liquidation of American securities by European holders. It caused a minor panic in this country, from which the Stock Exchange quickly recovered. European capital continued to leave the country, however; between 1890 and 1896, European repatriation of American investments averaged about $60 million a year. The withdrawal of foreign capital at a time when American industries were overexpanded was probably the immediate cause of the crash. In itself, however, the panic in Europe would not have caused a major depression in America. It merely exposed weaknesses that were already present.

None of these influences—the overexpansion of railroads and other industries, the weakness of the banking system, the agricultural depression and the decline of purchasing power, the European panic—appealed to the American people in 1893 as offering an explanation of their difficulties. Discussion fastened instead on the money question. No doubt the Democrats were correct in pointing out that widespread speculation in bullion and silver stocks had followed the enactment of the Sherman Silver Purchase Act, and that [widespread speculation], together with the rush to purchase commodities in expectation of rising prices under the McKinley tariff, caused a severe money stringency. They were doubtless correct in claiming that the purchase of great quantities of silver had made conservative businessmen tremble for the safety of the gold standard. Where they erred was in supposing that these facts told the whole story. Cleveland, addressing a special session of Congress on August 8, 1893, reviewed the "unfortunate plight" in which the nation found itself and roundly declared, "I believe these things are principally chargeable to Congressional legislation touching the purchase and coinage of silver by the General Government." Accordingly, he asked for "prompt repeal" of the Silver Purchase Act of 1890. This, it appeared, was the only immediate answer to the depression which the administration had to offer. That it was not enough the history of the next four years was to make painfully clear. . . .

Judged by almost any standard, the financial policy of the second Cleveland administration was a failure. Politically it split the party. It accomplished only one of the objectives Cleveland had set for himself; the gold standard, it is true, was successfully maintained, but not through repeal of the Sherman

Act, which was designed to save gold by easing the drain on the Treasury reserve. So far as the Treasury reserve was concerned, the repeal of the Sherman Act was a conspicuous failure. As for reduction of the tariff, nothing of any importance had been accomplished. Nor did the policies of the Cleveland administration alleviate the depression; it deepened in 1894 and, after a brief upturn in 1895, again in 1896. Not until late in 1897 did recovery begin. To Cleveland's disgust, the Republicans then claimed credit for it; their victory in 1896, they argued, had saved the country from the horrible prospect of free silver and brought renewed confidence to the business world.

". . . A crushing weight has been lifted and rolled away" [wrote *Dun's Review* . . . November 7, 1896], "and the business world has begun to adjust itself to a state of freedom and security which it has not known for years. Dread of immeasurable disaster no longer locks up resources and paralyzes enterprise, and new contracts involving many millions have become binding since the election. . . ."

But if the Republicans believed that by restoring confidence in the gold standard they had restored prosperity, they had forgotten that Cleveland had spent four years trying to save the gold standard and had in fact succeeded in saving it—his one indisputable achievement. The gold standard was already secure by the time the Republicans came to office. Yet the country was no closer to recovery in 1896 than it had been in 1893. The defense of gold, in short, did not bring recovery, a fact which shows that other causes were far more important in bringing on the depression than excessive anxiety over the currency. If the currency had been the real issue, Cleveland would have left office acclaimed as a hero instead of defeated and forlorn, despised by half his party, discarded by the other half as a political liability, and regarded by large numbers of his countrymen as a man who had sold them out to the House of Morgan.

unit three

The Great Depression, 1929-1939

The depressions of the 1840's and of the 1890's were two of the most severe in American history, but worst of them all was the one which began in 1929, known as the Great Depression. Like the American Revolution and the Civil War, it is one of the most significant events in United States history. The character of the American people, the nature of their institutions, and the course of their national development were profoundly altered by all three events. The effect of the American Revolution was mainly political. The Civil War and the Great Depression brought about fundamental social and economic changes as well.

The Great Depression caused the most dramatic economic decline in the history of the United States. In the process it destroyed the easy optimism that had developed during the first one hundred fifty years of the nation. It even altered basic beliefs among the people about the proper roles of government, business, and the individual citizen. Before the depression, government had exercised very limited control over economic affairs; business had been relatively free to operate as it wished; and each person was expected to look out for his own welfare. But the Great Depression convinced many Americans that not all persons could provide for themselves, especially when their livelihood depended upon a vast industrial system over which they had no control. As a result of popular demand during the 1930's, government took a more positive attitude toward aid and extended its assistance in many new ways.

To many persons, intervention in the market economy may have seemed unwise. Before a balanced judgment on this question is possible, one must first understand the flushed and hectic prosperity of the 1920's and the dark and terrible decade of the 1930's. In prosperous times it was difficult to imagine that the economy of the United States could deteriorate. Between 1931 and 1934, however, the United States did not create enough capital to replace the buildings and machines that were worn out from use or had decayed from idleness. During these years America became progressively less able to provide for its population.

The best indicator of national well-being is real income per capita, that is, the total amount of goods and services available as income for each person in a given year. Through the latter half of the nineteenth century real income had grown at an average annual rate of 1¾ per cent. Between 1929 and 1939, however, real income per capita did not increase at all, and at the bottom of the depression, in March 1933, it fell to the level of income in 1900. During the Great Depression, the course of American economic development stopped for a full decade.

The loss of material capital was overshadowed by the loss of human resources. The lives of millions, drawn from every age group and from every walk of life, were blighted during these years. Children suffered from inadequate food, slum housing, and poor education. Young adults saw their best years slip by in helpless futility and watched as old people died in desolation.

The psychological impact of the depression, coming as it did after the boom years of the 1920's, was enormous. After a short depression in the early 1920's the country had entered into a sustained prosperity lasting from 1922 to 1929. During this period of rapid industrial expansion, especially in the automotive, electrochemical, and electronics industries, real income per capita rose steadily. In 1921 it was $522; in 1929 it was $716, an increase of 37 per cent in eight years. Because of this rapid increase in wealth, men came to believe that America had a permanent hold on prosperity.

While optimism abounded, a more critical eye might have seen a flaw here and there. Large groups of people did not share in the prosperity. Farmers had expanded production in response to the demands of World War I. During the 1920's they faced the problem of chronic surpluses. The rise of the oil and electrical industries resulted in a decline in coal mining; the use of synthetic fibers in textile manufacturing hurt cotton farmers and sheep raisers. In addition, dozens of smaller industries were in continuous depression throughout the 1920's, and there seemed to be little interest in helping them. Once the long decline began, the sick industries helped speed and widen the deterioration of the others.

As the economic crisis deepened, a remarkable political upheaval took place. Crucial to the story of the Great Depression is the emergence of Franklin D. Roosevelt. His New Deal acted as a powerful force in producing the kind of society that followed the depression.

No one book could deal adequately with the vast panorama of the 1930's. In the brief compass of this volume, only a few of the most important events will be covered. Problem 11 looks at the statistical indicators of the economy in the 1920's and 1930's. Problem 12 traces the history of the stock market crash. Problem 13 investigates the social consequences of the depression, and Problem 14 examines the role of government during the decade after 1929. Problem 15 consists of an interpretation of the cause of the depression by a well-known economist.

PROBLEM 11

The Economy in the 1920's and the 1930's

The argument about the cause of the depression of the 1930's has been going on since the stock market crash of October 1929 first echoed down the narrow canyon of Wall Street. Much of the argument hinges on a single question: how sound was the American economy in the 1920's? During the late 1920's, before the crash, stockbrokers, politicians, and economists assured the public that the economy was sound, but their assurances were not supported by reliable interpretations of statistics. Economic statistics are indicators that show, to some degree, the health of an economy. In order to make sound judgments about the economy, a proper interpretation of the indicators is required.

Evidence regarding some important economic activities, such as manu- facturing, agriculture, and transportation, and their relationship to one an- other is given in the tables that make up Problem 11. The series is similar to that in Problem 6, Unit Two. Once again, as in Problem 6, you are to use the data provided by the tables to formulate hypotheses. However, in this Problem the focus is on the causes of the depression rather than on its effects as in Problem 6. Thus, although the depression began in 1929 and lasted through most of the 1930's, most of the data given cover the period from

1920 to 1933. As you study the tables in Problem 11, keep in mind these questions:

1   What parts of the economy of the 1920's were sound and what parts were not?

2   Compare levels of production in important sectors of the economy. What relation do you find between production and the rise and fall of the stock market? What relation is there between production and wages and prices? between production and distribution of income?

ECONOMIC INDICATORS OF THE 1920's

The following tables are from a volume prepared by the Bureau of the Census, with the advice and assistance of the Committee on Historical Statistics. The pages from which the tables are taken are shown with the tables.
☐ *Historical Statistics of the United States; Colonial Times to 1957.* Washington, D.C.: United States Bureau of the Census, 1960.

GROSS NATIONAL PRODUCT, TOTAL AND PER CAPITA

Gross National Product, or GNP, means the total market value of all goods and services produced in an economy.

1   What happened to GNP during the 1920's? to GNP per capita?

2   Using the data, what hypothesis can you make about the general standard of living of the entire population?

TABLE 1

Year	Total Gross National Product *in billions of dollars*	Gross National Product per capita *in dollars*
1920	$ 88.9	$ 835
1921	74.0	682
1922	74.0	672
1923	86.1	769
1924	87.6	768
1925	91.3	788
1926	97.7	832
1927	96.3	809
1928	98.2	815
1929	104.4	857
1930	91.1	740
1931	76.3	615
1932	58.5	468
1933	56.0	446

Historical Statistics, p. 139.
Current prices.

WHOLESALE PRICE INDEXES

The price indexes in Table 2 indicate the relative wholesale price of commodities for the years 1920 to 1933.

1   What was happening to prices during the 1920's?

2   Do these data confirm the hypothesis you made from Table 1? If not, how would you revise your hypothesis?

TABLE 2

Year	All commodities	All commodities except farm products and foods	Farm products
1920	100.3	115.3	84.2
1921	63.4	75.0	49.4
1922	62.8	73.2	52.4
1923	65.4	74.6	55.1
1924	63.8	71.3	55.9
1925	67.3	73.4	61.3
1926	65.0	71.5	55.9
1927	62.0	67.2	55.5
1928	62.9	66.4	59.2
1929	61.9	65.5	58.6
1930	56.1	60.9	49.3
1931	47.4	53.6	36.2
1932	42.1	50.2	26.9
1933	42.8	50.9	28.7

Historical Statistics, p. 117.
1947–1949 = 100.

HOURS AND EARNINGS FOR PRODUCTION WORKERS IN MANUFACTURING

Figures in Table 3 indicate the earnings of workers in manufacturing industries during the boom and the panic that followed.

1   When were wages going up?

2   Compare Tables 1 and 3. Were wages rising as rapidly as GNP per capita between 1921 and 1929? What hypothesis can you make about the way in which income was being distributed? If prices remained stable and manufacturing wages rose slowly, who got the major benefit from the increased productivity?

TABLE 3

Year	Average hourly earnings	Average weekly hours	Average weekly earnings
1920	$ .555	47.4	$ 26.30
1921	.515	43.1	22.18
1922	.487	44.2	21.51
1923	.522	45.6	23.82
1924	.547	43.7	23.93

TABLE 3 – Continued

Year	Average hourly earnings	Average weekly hours	Average weekly earnings
1925	.547	44.5	24.37
1926	.548	45.0	24.65
1927	.550	45.0	24.74
1928	.562	44.4	24.97
1929	.566	44.2	25.03
1930	.552	42.1	23.25
1931	.515	40.5	20.87
1932	.446	38.3	17.05
1933	.442	38.1	16.73

Historical Statistics, p. 92.

CORPORATION INCOME

Gross Income represents the total income received by corporations, and *Net Income* denotes total income minus cost of operations, cost of goods sold, and the deficits suffered by some corporations.

1   What happened to gross income of corporations from 1920 to 1933? to net income? to dividends paid to stockholders on common stock?

2   What hypothesis can you develop in regard to the income of wage earners (Table 3) compared to the income of owners of common stocks?

TABLE 4

Year	Total compiled receipts of gross income in thousands of dollars	Net income Surplus (+) Deficit (−) in thousands of dollars	Dividends paid to owners of common stock in thousands of dollars
1920	$ 118,205,562	$+5,873,231	*no data*
1921	91,249,274	+ 457,829	*no data*
1922	100,920,515	+4,770,035	$ 6,784,765
1923	119,019,865	+6,307,974	5,060,403
1924	119,746,703	+5,362,726	4,849,349
1925	134,779,997	+7,621,056	5,733,906
1926	142,629,445	+7,504,693	6,702,942
1927	144,899,177	+6,510,145	7,125,678
1928	153,304,973	+8,226,617	7,632,851
1929	161,158,206	+8,739,758	9,808,455
1930	136,588,320	+1,551,218	8,598,421
1931	108,056,952	− 3,287,545	6,314,614
1932	81,637,988	− 5,643,574	4,028,678
1933	84,234,006	− 2,547,367	3,229,502

Historical Statistics, p. 714.

VOLUME OF SALES AND PRICES OF COMMON STOCK

Table 5 gives three sets of data about the stock market in the period from 1920 to 1933: the volume of stock sales, the relative prices of stocks, and the per cent yield.

Per cent yield is determined by dividing total dividends paid by total stock values.

1   What happened to stock prices during the 1920? Were they rising more rapidly than GNP (Table 1)?

2   What could be a reason for the rapid rise in prices of stocks in industrials, railroads, and utilities after 1926 when the per cent yield on these investments was falling?

TABLE 5

Year	Volume of stock sales *in millions of shares*	Industrials		Railroads		Utilities	
		price index[1]	per cent yield	price index[1]	per cent yield	price index[1]	per cent yield
1920	227	31	5.54	47	6.81	22	8.06
1921	173	24	5.84	46	7.08	24	8.29
1922	259	30	5.37	52	5.95	29	7.62
1923	236	31	5.40	51	6.29	30	7.59
1924	282	32	5.25	55	6.44	33	7.35
1925	454	41	4.75	63	5.66	39	6.13
1926	451	48	5.24	71	5.52	41	5.57
1927	577	59	4.72	83	4.89	47	4.96
1928	920	79	3.82	95	4.76	62	4.09
1929	1,125	100	3.65	100	4.29	100	2.29
1930	810	77	4.45	86	5.27	90	3.19
1931	577	49	5.82	51	6.89	63	4.43
1932	425	25	6.58	19	5.30	35	7.36
1933	655	36	3.56	28	2.50	33	6.27

Historical Statistics, pp. 656, 659.
[1]1929 = 100.

INDICATORS OF ECONOMIC ACTIVITY

Table 6 shows data on the value of private and public construction, the value of finished commodities, and an index of manufacturing production.

1   When did the value of construction start to decline? When did the value of consumers' goods and producers' goods begin to decline or to level off?

2 From the evidence gathered from this table together with that in previous tables, what hypothesis can you make about the relative health of the economy?

TABLE 6—Part A

Year	Residential construction (nonfarm) *in millions of dollars*	Non-residential construction *in millions of dollars*	Farm construction *in millions of dollars*
1920	$ 2,015	$ 1,964	$ 566
1921	2,105	1,434	223
1922	3,360	1,457	269
1923	4,400	1,697	317
1924	5,060	1,675	298
1925	5,515	2,060	311
1926	5,600	2,513	297
1927	5,160	2,534	355
1928	4,770	2,573	331
1929	3,625	2,694	307
1930	2,075	2,003	193
1931	1,565	1,099	97
1932	630	502	37
1933	470	406	49

TABLE 6—Part B

Year	Consumers' semidurable goods[1] *in millions of dollars*	Consumers' durable goods[2] *in millions of dollars*	Producers' durable goods[3] *in millions of dollars*	Index of manufacturing production[4]
1920	$ 7,873	$ 4,899	$ 5,277	39
1921	5,632	3,270	2,939	30
1922	6,314	4,057	2,964	39
1923	7,230	5,367	4,396	45
1924	6,401	5,034	3,949	43
1925	7,134	5,786	4,256	48
1926	7,296	6,109	4,668	50
1927	7,391	5,436	4,320	50
1928	7,383	5,936	4,663	52
1929	7,458	6,312	5,628	58
1930	6,069	4,273	4,328	48
1931	4,931	3,252	2,628	39
1932	3,426	2,047	1,399	30
1933	3,773	2,321	1,487	36

Historical Statistics, pp. 379, 409, 419, 420, 421.
[1] Goods that can be used up, such as food.
[2] Goods such as home furnishings and cars, not used to produce other goods.
[3] Goods such as factory equipment, used to produce other goods.
[4] 1947–1949 = 100.

ESTIMATED ANNUAL POPULATION AND IMMIGRATION

During the second half of the nineteenth century, immigration had been encouraged by many groups in the United States, especially by industry and the railroads. American workers objected to the influx of cheap labor, and between 1882 and 1924, Congress passed a series of laws that made entry into the United States increasingly difficult. These laws largely accounted for a decline in immigration. The figures in Table 7 show statistics on immigration during the 1920's and early 1930's.

1   What happened to immigration and the rate of population increase during this period?

2   What hypothesis can you develop to relate the rate of population growth to the data in Table 6?

TABLE 7

Year	Estimated total population	Estimated total immigration	Annual percentage increase in population[1]
1920	106,466,000	430,001	1.86
1921	108,541,000	805,228	1.93
1922	110,055,000	309,556	1.39
1923	111,950,000	522,919	1.71
1924	114,113,000	706,896	1.93
1925	115,832,000	294,314	1.51
1926	117,399,000	304,488	1.37
1927	119,038,000	335,175	1.38
1928	120,501,000	307,355	1.23
1929	121,770,000	279,678	1.05
1930	123,077,000	241,700	1.07
1931	124,040,000	97,139	.78
1932	124,840,000	35,576	.64
1933	125,579,000	23,068	.59

Historical Statistics, pp. 7, 56.
[1]Calculated from estimated total population.

GOVERNMENT SPENDING AND THE DEPRESSION

Table 8 shows data on federal revenues, expenditures, deficits, and unemployment.

1   How does government revenue compare to government expenditure during the period shown? Did government expenditure rise as unemployment increased?

2   Do these data substantiate the hypothesis you made from Table 6? If not, how would you revise that hypothesis?

TABLE 8

Year	Government revenue *in billions of dollars*	Government expenditure *in billions of dollars*	Surplus (+) Deficit (−) *in billions of dollars*	Number of unemployed *number in millions*	Per cent of labor force unemployed
1920	$ 6.69	$ 6.40	$+ .29	1.67	4.0
1921	5.62	5.12	+ .50	5.01	11.9
1922	4.11	3.37	+ .74	3.22	7.6
1923	4.01	3.30	+ .71	1.38	3.2
1924	4.01	3.09	+ .92	2.44	5.5
1925	3.78	3.06	+ .72	1.8	4.0
1926	3.96	3.10	+ .86	.88	1.9
1927	4.13	2.97	+1.16	1.89	4.1
1928	4.04	3.10	+ .94	2.08	4.4
1929	4.03	3.30	+ .73	1.55	3.2
1930	4.18	3.44	+ .74	4.34	8.7
1931	3.19	3.58	− .39	8.02	15.9
1932	2.01	4.66	− 2.65	12.06	23.6
1933	2.08	4.62	− 2.54	12.83	24.9

Historical Statistics, pp. 73, 712, 718.

PROBLEM 12

The Stock Market Crash

The stock market crash of 1929 signaled the end of the boom years of the 1920's. Nothing in the entire decade was so dramatic nor had such absolutely dismal results as the crash. October 24 and 29, sometimes referred to as Black Thursday and Tragic Tuesday, ended the boom and ushered in a decade of the severest depression the nation had ever known. It also brought in years of sobering maturity.

The stock market, or stock exchange, was far more central to American life in the 1920's than it ever was before. The affairs of giant corporations shared newspaper space with heroes of the time, such as Charles A. Lindbergh, the first aviator to fly solo across the Atlantic Ocean, and George Herman "Babe" Ruth, the home-run king of baseball. The stock market had attracted one out of every eighty Americans. More than 1,500,000 persons owned shares of stock, a number large enough to make the market a familiar topic of conversation. The jargon of the market entered everyday speech; men who made fortunes buying and selling stocks became folk heroes.

Stocks represent shares of ownership in corporations. When a corporation wishes to raise money, it may offer stock for sale on the market. Each person who buys a share of stock thereby purchases part ownership in the corporation. Each share usually entitles a shareholder to one vote in the affairs of the company, to be exercised at annual meetings.

Some companies distribute their profits among stockholders in the form of dividends, which might be paid in money or in added shares of stock. Many times companies do not pay dividends, but if the price of a company's stock rises, stockholders may sell it for more than they paid for it and thus make a profit.

When prices of stocks rise, the market is called a "bull market." When prices fall, it is a "bear market." The prices of some stocks rise when a demand for those particular stocks occurs. Sometimes people are willing to pay higher prices for a stock because a company is paying high dividends. At other times buyers may be interested in the stock of a company that has used its profits to expand its business and modernize its equipment and thus would be likely to make more money in the future.

But neither of these considerations lay behind the rising prices of the big bull market of the 1920's. During those hectic years, many men bought stocks on the assumption that prices would continue to rise indefinitely. As long as men continued to buy and prices went up, no one could lose; in fact everyone *could* get rich. But what would happen if prices fell?

The situation was complicated by the practice of buying on margin. This kind of purchase meant that a buyer would make a partial payment on the stock he was buying, with a promise to pay for, or protect, the remaining amount if necessary. As long as the price of his stock rose, he had no difficulty because he could sell his shares for a larger sum than the purchase price and make a handsome profit in the process. However, if prices fell below his purchase price and he had to borrow money to protect his account, he could lose not only his partial payment but also what he borrowed. In many instances men faced bankruptcy after buying stock on margin.

The big bull market began in 1927. Except for two brief dips, the price of major stocks rose steadily. Voices of caution were not loud enough to be heard over the jubilance of those who were expecting to make great fortunes. There was a major break in June, but prices continued up through 1928, particularly late in the year. Although signs indicated early in 1929 that speculation was exceedingly dangerous, neither the financiers of Wall Street nor the federal government took decisive steps to end it. The rise in prices stopped early in September. Prices slipped downward, then up, and continued to fluctuate, but there were no dramatic breaks in the market until October 23. Then prices started to sink rapidly. The crash was at hand.

The readings in Problem 12 examine the history of the crash itself. As you read, keep the following questions in mind:

1   What caused the stock market crash?

2   The stock market crash had obvious, immediate effects on speculators and investors. What were the possibilities of its long-range effects on other Americans?

3   How was the big bull market related to income distribution in the 1920's as indicated by Table 3 in Problem 11?

I

BLACK THURSDAY AND TRAGIC TUESDAY

Thursday, October 24, 1929, has become known as an infamous day in financial history. Actually, it marked only the end of the boom. The tragedy had been long in the making, starting with the beginning of wild speculation "to get rich quick." The following excerpt describes the beginning of the stock market crash of 1929. □ *The New York Times,* October 25, 1929, pp. 1–2. Copyright © 1929 by The New York Times Company. Reprinted by permission.

WORST STOCK CRASH STEMMED BY BANKS; 12,894,650-SHARE DAY SWAMPS MARKET; LEADERS CONFER, FIND CONDITIONS SOUND

Losses Recovered in Part

Upward Trend Starts with 200,000-Share Order for Steel

Tickers Lag Four Hours

Thousands of Accounts Wiped Out, With Traders in Dark as to Events on Exchange

Sales on Curb 6,337,415

Prices on Markets in Other Cities Also Slump and Rally
—Wheat Values Hard Hit.

The most disastrous decline in the biggest and broadest stock market of history rocked the financial district yesterday. In the very midst of the collapse five of the country's most influential bankers hurried to the office of J. P. Morgan & Co., and after a brief conference gave out word that they believe the foundations of the market to be sound, that the market smash has been caused by technical rather than fundamental considerations, and that many sound stocks are selling too low.

Suddenly the market turned about, on buying orders thrown into the pivotal issues, and before the final quotations were tapped out, four hours and eight minutes after the 3 o'clock bell, most stocks had regained a measurable part of their losses.

LOSSES AT CLOSE NOT EXCESSIVE.

The break was one of the widest in the market's history, although the losses at the close were not particularly large, many having been recouped by the afternoon rally.

It carried down with it speculators, big and little, in every part of the country, wiping out thousands of accounts. It is probable that if the stockholders of the country's foremost corporations had not been calmed by the attitude of leading bankers and the subsequent rally, the business of the country would have been seriously affected. Doubtless business will feel the effects of the drastic stock shake-out, and this is expected to hit the luxuries most severely. . . .

THOUSANDS SACRIFICE HOLDINGS.

The total losses cannot be accurately calculated, because of the large number of markets and the thousands of securities not listed on any exchange. However, they were staggering, running into billions of dollars. Fear struck the big speculators and little ones, big investors and little ones. Thousands of them threw their holdings into the whirling Stock Exchange pit for what they would bring. Losses were tremendous and thousands of prosperous brokerage and bank accounts, sound and healthy a week ago, were completely wrecked in the strange debacle, due to a combination of circumstances, but accelerated into a crash by fear. . . .

FINANCIAL DISTRICT IN CONFUSION.

Under these circumstances of late tickers and spreads of 10, 20 and at times 30 points between the tape prices and those on the floor of the Exchange, the entire financial district was thrown into hopeless confusion and excitement. Wild-eyed speculators crowded the brokerage offices, awed by the disaster which had overtaken many of them. They followed the market literally "in the dark," getting but meager reports via the financial news tickers which printed the Exchange floor prices at ten-minute intervals.

Rumors, most of them wild and false, spread throughout the Wall Street district and thence throughout the country. One of the reports was that eleven speculators had committed suicide. A peaceful workman atop a Wall Street building looked down and saw a big crowd watching him, for the rumor had spread that he was going to jump off. Reports that the Chicago and Buffalo Exchanges had closed spread throughout the district, as did rumors that the New York Stock Exchange and the New York Curb Exchange were going to suspend trading. These rumors and reports were all found, on investigation, to be untrue. . . .

It was not the calm slipping away of stocks as had been the case in many previous markets. By 11 o'clock it had become a wild scramble, with "sell at the market" resounding in every brokerage office in the country and the effect was perhaps the most astonishing crash of open market values that the Street has ever seen. If there was any support in the market at all, it was swept forcibly aside, as leading stocks crashed down and down by 1 point, 2 points, and even 5 and 10 between sales as the violence increased. . . .

Margins by the thousands became exhausted and frightened stockholders in all parts of the country seemed to have become terror stricken. Ineffectual attempts to keep Steel above 200 proved unsuccessful, although there was a short, sharp battle around the Steel post because of the general knowledge that if Steel crashed through 200 it would exert a tremendously disquieting effect on the balance of the market. But crash through it did, and before the market was saved from itself the market leader, which had opened at 205½, had smashed its way down to 194½. . . .

Stocks were thrown in, in tremendous volume, for just what they would bring at forced sale. The greatest damage and the lowest prices were reached between 11:15 and 12:15. Soon after that time, leading bankers were observed enroute to the offices of J. P. Morgan & Co. With the knowledge that a statement would soon be made from the Morgan offices, the Street guessed that it would relate to market support. There was an immediate turnabout in stocks, and the leaders started their fast climb up the ladder of fluctuations, down which they had so ingloriously tumbled an hour before.

Although influential Wall Street bankers professed confidence in the soundness of the market, the decline in prices continued. On October 29, 1929, in another stock collapse, the third of the week, millions more shares were dumped for whatever they would bring. Bankers continued to be optimistic, believing that the rush to liquidate stocks had by that day run its course.

However, Tragic Tuesday ushered in the worst depression in the history of the United States. □ *The New York Times,* October 30, 1929, pp. 1–2. Copyright © 1929 by The New York Times Company. Reprinted by permission.

From every point of view, in the extent of losses sustained, in total turnover, in the number of speculators wiped out, the day was the most disastrous in Wall Street's history. Hysteria swept the country and stocks went overboard for just what they would bring at forced sale.

Efforts to estimate yesterday's market losses in dollars are futile because of the vast number of securities quoted over the counter and on out-of-town exchanges on which no calculations are possible. However, it was estimated that 880 issues, on the New York Stock Exchange. lost between $8,000,000,000 and $9,000,000,000 yesterday. . . .

Banking support, which would have been impressive and successful under ordinary circumstances, was swept violently aside, as block after block of stock, tremendous in proportions, deluged the market. Bid prices placed by bankers, industrial leaders and brokers trying to halt the decline were crashed through violently, their orders were filled, and quotations plunged downward in a day of disorganization, confusion and financial impotence.

CHANGE IS EXPECTED TODAY.

That there will be a change today seemed likely from statements made last night by financial and business leaders. Organized support will be accorded to the market from the start, it is believed, but those who are staking their all on the country's leading securities are placing a great deal of confidence, too, in the expectation that there will be an overnight change in sentiment; that the counsel of cool heads will prevail and that the mob psychology which has been so largely responsible for the market's debacle will be broken. . . .

Yesterday's market crash was one which largely affected rich men, institutions, investment trusts and others who participate in the stock market on a broad and intelligent scale. It was not the margin traders who were caught in the rush to sell, but the rich men of the country who are able to swing blocks of 5,000, 10,000 up to 100,000 shares of high-priced stocks. They went overboard with no more consideration [for them] than [for] the little trader who was swept out on the first day. . . .

The market on the rampage is no respecter of persons. It washed fortune after fortune away yesterday and financially crippled thousands of individuals in all parts of the world. It was not until after the market had closed that the financial district began to realize that a good-sized rally had taken place and that there was a stopping place on the downgrade for good stocks.

The market has now passed through three days of collapse, and so violent has it been that most authorities believe that the end is not far away. . . .

Sentiment had been generally unsettled since the first of September. Market prices had then reached peak levels, and, try as they would, pool operators and other friends of the market could not get them higher. It was a gradual downward sag, gaining momentum as it went on, then to break out into an open market smash in which the good, the bad and indifferent stocks went down alike. Thousands of traders were able to weather the first storm and answered their margin calls; thousands fell by the wayside Monday and again yesterday, unable to meet the demands of their brokers that their accounts be protected.

There was no quibbling at all between customer and broker yesterday. In any case where margin became thin a peremptory call went out. If there was not immediate answer the stock was sold out "at the market" for just what it would bring. Thousands, sold out on the decline and amid the confusion, found themselves in debt to their brokers last night.

II

HOW THE INSIDERS OPERATED

During the late 1920's thousands of men and women began to buy and sell stocks for the first time in their lives. Lacking experience, they were often sheared like lambs by the insiders, who were brokers and members of exchanges with access to first-hand information which they used to their own advantage. The following account reveals some of the practices of one brokerage house in 1928. □ Robert Ryan, "Brokers and 'Suckers.'" New York: *The Nation,* Volume 127, Number 3293, August 15, 1928, pp. 154–156.

During the spring months of this year the customers' rooms of Wall Street's brokerage houses were overflowing with a new type of speculator. In these broad rooms you could see feverish young men and heated elders, eyes intent upon the ticker tape. The ranks of the inexperienced—the "suckers"— were swelled by numbers of men who had been attracted by newspaper stories of the big, easy profits to be made in a tremendous bull market, of millions captured overnight by the Fisher Brothers, Arthur Cutten, and [William C.] Durant. At first these newcomers risked a few hundred dollars with some broker they knew, discovered that it was easy to make money this way, and finally made their headquarters in the broker's large customers' room, bringing with them their entire checking and savings accounts.

These amateurs were not schooled in markets that had seen stringent, panicky drops in prices. They came in on a rising tide. They speculated on tips, on hunches, on "follow-the-leader" principles. When a stock rose sharply they all jumped for it—and frequently were left holding the bag of higher prices. They would sell or buy on the slightest notice, usually obeying implicitly the advice of their broker.

Out of this combustible desire to trade in and out of the market, abuses have arisen. Some brokers, none too scrupulous, have taken advantage of the helplessness of the small customer. The broker can make more commissions by rapid trading than by holding stocks for real appreciation in value, and he knows that this particular type of customer is here today and gone tomorrow. He must make commissions while the money shines.

Sometime ago I spent about two months in a busy broker's office. I had been offered a position as customer's man (to get new accounts and keep them posted on the market's doings). As I wanted to see whether I would like this work, I asked for a two months' period in which to learn the business. The broker with whom I became associated is considered reliable and honest, and the offer was supposedly an attractive one. I sat in the private office of the president and was thus able to follow quite minutely the methods by which he conducted his business. Years of experience with ordinary business had given me no hint of the practices I saw occur as everyday procedure —in the main practices highly prejudicial to the average customer's interest. So astonished was I that I questioned several other Wall Street brokers, only to find that the practices I saw were common enough on the Street, indulged in more or less generally by large and small firms.

There are two ways in which stock may be bought through a broker. One is to limit the price by stipulating exactly what the broker may pay. For instance, if you wished to buy General Motors stock, you would see on the ticker tape that the last quoted sale was at $194 a share. If you were willing to pay that price or less you would order your broker to buy 50 shares at $194. In this way, if the price had jumped a point or so after the quotation you saw, you would not buy the stock, but your order would stand at $194 until you got the stock at that price or canceled the order. It might also happen that if the stock had a temporary recession, you would get it at less than $194 a share.

The other method of buying is to give a "market order." Thus, in the same circumstances as those above, if General Motors had a sudden rise in price you would pay the current rate being quoted on the Stock Exchange floor. It might be $194.50, $196, or more, as the stock responded to buying. Or if the stock were selling for less, you would also pay the current quotation. When placing a market order you cannot tell what price you will pay for your stock.

I shall list here a few of the incidents I witnessed while in the office. On Thursday the partner of Mr. X . . . had bought some shares of Arabian bank stock at $440 a share. This stock was not listed on the Stock Exchange but was dealt in by over-the-counter houses (houses which deal in unlisted securities). These firms make their own prices, determined solely by the demand for the stock. There is usually a marked difference in quotations by these houses, and the practice is to call several of them before buying in order to get the best price. On Friday morning a customer of Mr. X telephoned an order to sell 50 shares of Arabian bank stock. Mr. X obtained his permission to sell "at the best price." He called to his partner, "Want any more of that Arabian bank stock?"

"At what price?" answered Mr. Y [the partner]. "I paid $440 a share yesterday."

"You can have this for less," said Mr. X. "I've got a market order. The market is 415 bid, 445 offered. Want it at 415?"

"Sure," said Mr. Y. And the customer was informed that it was too bad he got such a low price—but after all, "we sold it at the market."

The dishonesty of this transaction lies in the fact that if several firms had been called and the stock offered for sale, a better price could have been obtained, for this was an active stock in good demand with a wide difference between the bid-and-ask prices.

Incident No. 2: This firm was "bullish" on a certain stock—they believed its price would go higher. Suddenly a panic developed in the stock and it began to decline at a rapid rate. The large and small customers who owned the stock all began selling at once. When the selling confirmations came in, Mr. X announced that no selling prices could be given out until all the orders were checked. In the next half hour Mr. X and his partners selected those sales which had brought the best prices, allotted these best prices to their larger customers, and allowed the small fry to get what was left. This is obviously unfair discrimination. A record is kept by the order clerk of the sequence in which the selling orders are placed. Consequently, the prices of the sales should have been allotted in that order. "Of course," Mr. X remarked, "we make the most money from our large customers . . . ."

Incident No. 3: The broker charges a standard—and substantial—commission on the orders he executes, yet it is common practice among all firms to borrow money at, let us say, 5 per cent and charge 6 per cent to their customers who buy on margin. The Stock Exchange has ruled that brokers may charge their customers the exact amount of interest, or more than the exact amount, that they themselves have to pay when they borrow the money in the open market or from banks; but in no case may brokers charge the customers *less* than the brokers pay in borrowing the money.

This rule has been promulgated in order that brokers may not offer the extra inducement of a reduced interest rate to large speculators in order to acquire them as customers. This rule does away with a great deal of cut-throat competition; but in practice the large customer is actually charged the same amount of interest as the broker pays or very little more, while the small customer pays an average of ¾ of one per cent additional on all money which he uses when buying on margin. This ¾ of one per cent, various brokers have told me, is intended to cover the entire overhead cost of their business. This means that the commissions which are paid for buying or selling the stock are net income to the brokerage house. It is easy to understand why brokerage houses insist that they are justified in charging this so-called "service fee" for negotiating a loan for a client. . . .

. . . [Another incident]: Mr. X advised all his customers to buy "Rotton Apples Common." Since Mr. X's firm helped to finance the stock issue their interest in selling this stock could hardly be wholly disinterested.

It would be simple to . . . cite other practices, but what I suggested in the first part of this article has, I believe, been . . . shown: in every case under my observation the broker felt that he must give the advantage, even though it were a dishonest advantage, to his large customer, for the large customer is his bread and butter and his profits. The small investor or speculator remains completely unaware of these practices. In a rising market such methods may be employed without losing the customer's business, for a speculator will overlook small irregularities as long as he continues to make money; while in a declining market the broker gets away with an equal amount of dishonesty, the customer blames the results on market drops. If a customer loses all his money, or so dislikes the actions of Mr. X's firm that he withdraws his business, Mr. X is completely unconcerned. As he remarked to me: "Suckers are born every minute; the glamor of easy money gets them all. One goes, two come in. Win or lose, we get our commissions." It is an easygoing philosophy which has been so completely proved true by many Wall Street brokers that they have no reason to revise it.

How such practices can be stopped I do not know; nor do I imagine that it is within the power of the Stock Exchange authorities to prevent them. I do believe that one step ahead would be to forbid all brokerage houses or their employees to transact business for themselves, to compel them to act solely as customers' agents. Surely this would make them a trifle more disinterested in the advice they give their clients.

In the meantime Mr. X's firm is making money hand over fist.

III

THE TRAGEDY SUMMARIZED

The author of the following excerpt was a former president of the National City Bank of New York. He said, "If I draw illustrations from the banking field to indicate the limits to which the depression reached, it is only because I am writing about banks and not because the banks are the one glaring example marking the extent of the financial cataclysm. The railroads, the insurance companies, the building and loan societies and mortgage companies would quite as well depict the situation." □ Frank A. Vanderlip, "What About the Banks?" *Saturday Evening Post*, Volume 205, Number 19, November 5, 1932, pp. 3–4. Reprinted by permission of Frank A. Vanderlip, Jr.

The present economic disturbance has been so severe that it has made even some changes in our language. No longer is it an apt metaphor to say that anything is "as safe as a bank." The word "securities" has almost become obsolete. An investment that drops in price to a tenth or, perhaps, even to a twentieth of its former range is not a security; it is a jeopardy. The page of stock-and-bond quotations might well be headed Quotations of Risks and Hazards. To call them securities in the light of their fluctuations is ironical.

In 1720, a financial debacle [concerning the South Sea Company] added to the English language a phrase which has persisted in common world-wide use for two centuries. A hopelessly exploded financial venture is to this day called a South Sea Bubble. . . .

Here is an example from our own times: United States Steel and General Motors stock, the two leading industrials of the country, declined from the high quotation of 1929 to 8 per cent of that price. The decline in the stock of the South Sea Company was only to 13½ per cent of its highest quotation. Take another example: The stock of what has long been one of the premier banks of the country declined from 585 to 23½. That is to say, it fell to 4 per cent of its highest quotation. The decline in the market price of this great American banking institution was . . . more than three times as severe as was the fall in the stock of the South Sea Company.

That illustration is by no means a unique one. There were innumerable American bank stocks which made a more distressing record. Between October 1, 1929, and August 31, 1932, 4835 American banks failed. They had deposits aggregating $3,263,049,000. The stocks of many of those banks not only fell to zero; some did worse than that, for they carried on to the shoulders of the stockholders further liability, which had to be met, in addition to the complete loss of the money which had been invested when the stocks were bought. . . .

The decline in the price of bank stocks was only a minor phase of our debacle. The quoted value of all stocks listed on the New York Stock Exchange was, on September 1, 1929, $89,668,276,854. By July 1, 1932, the quoted value of all stocks had fallen to $15,633,479,577.

Stockholders had lost $74,000,000,000. This figure is so large that not many minds can grasp it. It is $616 for every one of us in America. It is, roughly, three times what we spent in fighting the World War. The bursting of the South Sea Bubble concerned a single company. In the bursting of the New York Stock Exchange bubble, the value of all stocks fell to 17 per cent of their September 1, 1929, price—almost as great a drop as the South Sea Company stock, with its fall to 13 per cent of its top price. Remember that this calculation is not a selected example. It is made from the average of all stocks listed on the Exchange.

The South Sea Bubble wasn't so much! We have done pretty well in the way of bubbles in our own time. All financial history shows no parallel to what we have been going through. Never before, in this country or anywhere else, has there been such a general loss in "security" values.

The decline in the quoted value of New York listed stocks is only part of the story. The total of real-estate mortgages in default, particularly mortgages on city property, is unexampled. The value of real estate can no longer be accurately appraised, because the market for real estate has been practically paralyzed. . . .

This is a shameful and humiliating exhibition. It is uniquely bad. Across the border in Canada, there was not a single bank failure during our period of depression, and one must go back to 1923 to find even a small one. Nowhere else in the world at any time, were it a time of war, or of famine, or of disaster, has any other people recorded so many bank failures in a similar period as did we. We were not experiencing a war, a famine or any other natural disaster. All the economic tribulations we have undergone in the past three years have been man-made troubles, and Nature has continued to shower us with an easy abundance—more, indeed, than we have known how to distribute with economic wisdom.

Human stupidity and cupidity were the taproots of this great financial disaster. Those are evils which will always beset us. There have, however, been revealed faults and weaknesses in our banking and investment practices that account in part for the extreme nature of this experience.

The Social Consequences
of the Depression

The stock market crash triggered a dismal general depression. The assurances of bankers, the last-minute attempt of a few of the wealthiest businessmen to bolster the market by large purchases, the optimistic speeches of the President—none had the least effect. Each day the troubles grew worse. Each week the breadlines grew longer. Each month more and more farms were sacrificed at auctions. The wheels of the American economy were slowly grinding to a halt.

Within a year after the stock market crash 6,000,000 men were unemployed. By 1932, the worst of the depression years, Chicago alone had more than 650,000 jobless; New York City counted over a million. During the three years after the crash an average of 100,000 workers were laid off from their jobs every week, and there were no new jobs to be found. In a number of industrial cities, well over half the labor force was unemployed. In Donora, Pennsylvania, a steel town with an obsolete plant, only 277 of 13,900 workers held regular jobs.

In the worst of the depression, fully a fourth of the labor force was unemployed. By 1932 manufacturing plants were producing only a little more than half of their 1929 output.

If anything, conditions were worse on the farms. The farmer had shared little in the prosperity of the 1920's. He began the decade in the midst of a disastrous fall of prices. In the single year, between 1920 and 1921, prices of farm products fell almost 60 per cent. Some crops, such as wheat, were hit even harder. Prices stayed low throughout the 1920's, partly because Europeans raised tariff barriers in response to high tariffs imposed by the United States. With the crash, prices collapsed again. Wheat fell from $1.05 a bushel in 1929 to 39 cents a bushel three years later. Other crops followed suit. Gross farm income was cut from $12 billion to $5 billion.

The depression touched everyone. Former stockbrokers and bankers sold apples or shined shoes on street corners. Lights dimmed over Broadway theaters. Baseball stars saw their salaries sliced to the bone as the stands yawned empty before them. The depression was truly a national calamity. It respected no social class, occupation, section, or profession.

The readings in Problem 13 examine some typical reactions to the depression by various people in different sections and occupations. As you read these accounts, keep the following questions in mind:

1 Whom did the depression strike harder—the farmer or the wage-earner?

2 Were the different reactions of Americans toward the depression influenced by their occupations?

3 Do you think unemployed Americans would have objected to federal relief in 1932?

4 Were farmers of the United States really overproducing in the early thirties, particularly 1931 and 1932?

I

OLE SWANSON, FARMER, LOSES HIS LIFE SAVINGS

The following article tells how Ole Swanson, a farmer, struggled through the depression years. His case was by no means unique—hundreds of thousands of other farmers were in the same predicament. ☐ Bernhard Ostrolenk, "The Farmer's Plight: A Far-Reaching Crisis." *The New York Times*, September 25, 1932, Section 8, p. 1. Copyright © 1932 by The New York Times Company. Reprinted by permission.

By 1912 Ole, then 35 years old and a renter, had accumulated some $2,000 in cash, two teams of horses, a reasonable supply of implements, a few brood sows and some cattle. He decided to buy his deceased father's farm of 160 acres in Southern Minnesota for $20,000. He paid $2,000 in cash, gave an $8,000 second mortgage to the estate and a $10,000 first mortgage to an insurance company.

Between 1912 and 1920, because of exceptional thrift and competence, Ole was able to pay off the entire second mortgage of $8,000, besides improving his barns, adding more cattle to his herd, increasing his equipment, building a porch to his home and making other improvements, as well as buying furniture, rugs and books, and giving his children an adequate education.

But between 1920 and 1928 Ole found that his expenses, because of the industrial prosperity, were increasing. He had to pay more and more for labor and for goods. On the other hand, because of the drop in agricultural prices, his income was constantly falling. So, in those years, he was unable to amortize his remaining $10,000 mortgage, and, moreover, found that his standard of living was rapidly declining. By 1925 his net income for his labor had fallen to less than $400 annually.

His 18-year-old daughter, who had become employed in town as a typist, with no experience whatever and without invested capital, was earning $15 a week, or nearly $800 a year, almost twice what Ole was earning for his labor during that period.

In 1929 Ole was unable to meet a total interest of $600 and taxes of $300 and was compelled to give the insurance company, holding his mortgage, a chattel mortgage for the interest debt. In 1930 he was compelled to give an even larger chattel mortgage.

In 1931 his gross income was insufficient to meet either taxes or interest, and the insurance company, now having failed to get interest for three years, foreclosed the mortgage in the Spring of 1932. Ole, at the age of 55, was again a renter on his father's farm—the farm upon which he had been born and on which he had labored for a quarter of a century; having lost his entire equity of $10,000, he was left carrying a burdensome chattel mortgage.

Ole's career exemplifies the trend of American agriculture today. Not all the farmers have been foreclosed, but all are carrying heavy burdens. A mortgage of $10,000 on a 160-acre farm means that the farmer must pay $3.60 interest per acre. His taxes amount to about $1.90 per acre, making a total funded debt of $5.50 per acre. But with oats selling at 10 cents a bushel, the forty bushels he may be able to raise per acre, if lucky, will give him less gross return than he needs for those purposes alone. Certainly there is nothing left for out-of-pocket expenses, such as binder twine and tool repair, labor, seed and interest on the equity which he himself has in the farm. . . . Ole, now a renter, has estimated that his gross income at present price levels will be about $800 for 1932. Instead of paying interest and taxes of $900, as he was expected to do last year before his foreclosure, he will now pay as rent to the insurance company that held his mortgage only one-third of his sales, or about $265.

Yet the average farmer is reluctant to surrender his status of independent farm owner even under such conditions. Though he becomes progressively poorer, he clings to the land as long as he can.

II

AN EDITOR DESCRIBES REACTIONS TO THE DEPRESSION

Oscar Ameringer, a magazine editor, toured the nation during the early 1930's and witnessed various reactions of victims of the depression. In a report to the House of Representatives he described the conditions he had seen in the states he visited. ☐ Hearings before a Subcommittee of the Committee on Labor, House of Representatives, 72nd Congress, 1st Session, on H.R. 206, H.R. 6011, H.R. 8088, pp. 98–99. Washington, D.C.: United States Congress, 1932.

During the last three months I have visited, as I have said, some 20 States of this wonderfully rich and beautiful country. Here are some of the things I heard and saw: In the State of Washington I was told that the forest fires raging in that region all summer and fall were caused by unemployed timber workers and bankrupt farmers in an endeavor to earn a few honest dollars as fire fighters. The last thing I saw on the night I left Seattle was numbers of women searching for scraps of food in the refuse piles of the principal market of that city. A number of Montana citizens told me of thousands of bushels of wheat left in the fields uncut on account of its low price that hardly paid for the harvesting. In Oregon I saw thousands of bushels of apples rotting in the orchards. Only . . . flawless apples were still salable at from 40 to 50 cents a box containing 200 apples. At the same time, there are millions of children who, on account of the poverty of their parents, will not eat one apple this winter.

While I was in Oregon the Portland Oregonian bemoaned the fact that thousands of ewes were killed by the sheep raisers because they did not bring enough in the market to pay the freight on them. And while Oregon sheep raisers fed mutton to the buzzards, I saw men picking for meat scraps in the garbage cans in the cities of New York and Chicago. I talked to one man in a restaurant in Chicago. He told me of his experience in raising sheep. He said he had killed 3,000 sheep this fall and thrown them down the canyon, because it cost $1.10 to ship a sheep, and then he would get less than a dollar for it. He said he could not afford to feed the sheep, and he would not let them starve, so he just cut their throats and threw them down the canyon.

The roads of the West and Southwest teem with hungry hitchhikers. The camp fires of the homeless are seen along every railroad track. I saw men, women, and children walking over the hard roads. Most of them were tenant farmers who had lost their all in the late slump in wheat and cotton. Between Clarksville and Russellville, Ark., I picked up a family. The woman was hugging a dead chicken under a ragged coat. When I asked her where she had procured the fowl, first she told me she had found it dead in the road, and then added in grim humor, "They promised me a chicken in the pot, and now I got mine."

In Oklahoma, Texas, Arkansas, and Louisiana I saw untold bales of cotton rotting in the fields because the cotton pickers could not keep body and soul together on 35 cents paid for picking 100 pounds. The farmers co-operatives who loaned the money to the planters to make the crops allowed the planters $5 a bale. That means 1,500 pounds of seed cotton for the picking of it, which was in the neighborhood of 35 cents . . . [per 100 pounds]. A good picker can pick about 200 pounds of cotton a day, so that the 70 cents would not provide enough pork and beans to keep the picker in the field, so that there is fine staple cotton rotting down there by the hundreds and thousands of tons.

As a result of this appalling overproduction on the one side and the staggering underconsumption on the other side, 70 per cent of the farmers of Oklahoma were unable to pay the interests on their mortgages. Last week one of the largest and oldest mortgage companies in that State went into the hands of the receiver. In that and other States we have now the interesting spectacle of farmers losing their farms by foreclosure and mortgage companies losing their recouped holdings by tax sales.

The farmers are being pauperized by the poverty of industrial populations and the industrial populations are being pauperized by the poverty of the farmers. Neither has the money to buy the product of the other, hence we have overproduction and underconsumption at the same time and in the same country.

I have not come here to stir you in a recital of the necessity for relief for our suffering fellow citizens. However, unless something is done for them and done soon, you will have a revolution on hand. And when that revolution comes it will not come from Moscow, it will not be made by the . . . communists whom our police are heading up regularly and efficiently. When the revolution comes it will bear the label "Laid in the U.S.A." and its chief promoters will be the people of American stock.

III

NEW WAYS TO LIVE IN THE CITY

Millions of men thrown out of work reacted to the depression in as many different ways. The following selection is from the columns of *The New York Times*. Its author describes how some men in New York City made jobs for themselves so that they could scrape together enough money to enable them to get by. □ Pat Frank, "Jobless Find New Ways To Make a Living." *The New York Times,* June 5, 1932, Section 9, p. 2. Copyright © 1932 by The New York Times Company. Reprinted by permission.

Darwin's theory that man can adapt himself to almost any new environment is being illustrated, in this day of economic change, by thousands of New Yorkers who have discovered new ways to live and new ways to earn a living since their formerly placid lives were thrown into chaos by unemployment or kindred exigencies. Occupations and duties which once were scorned have suddenly attained unprecedented popularity. . . .

FIVE CENTS—AND NO TIP.

Once the average New Yorker got his shine in an established bootblack "parlor" paying 10 cents, with a nickel tip. But now, in the Times Square and Grand Central zones, the sidewalks are lined with neophyte "shine boys," drawn from almost all walks of life. They charge a nickel, and although a nickel tip is welcomed it is not expected.

In one block, on West Forty-third Street, a recent count showed nineteen shoe-shiners. They ranged in age from a 16-year-old, who should have been in school, to a man of more than 70, who said he had been employed in a fruit store until six months ago. Some sit quietly on their little wooden boxes and wait patiently for the infrequent customers. Others show true initiative and ballyhoo their trade, pointing accusingly at every pair of unshined shoes that passes. . . .

Shining shoes, said one, is more profitable than selling apples—and he's tried them both.

THE COST OF EQUIPMENT.

"You see, when you get a shine kit it's a permanent investment," he said, "and it doesn't cost as much as a box of apples anyway. . . ."

According to the Police Department, there are approximately 7,000 of these "shine boys" making a living on New York streets at present. Three years ago they were so rare as to be almost non-existent, and were almost entirely boys under 17.

To the streets, too, has turned an army of new salesmen, peddling everything from large rubber balls to cheap neckties. Within the past two years the number of these hawkers has doubled. Some are peddlers by profession, but others are former salesmen of more stable goods who have decided to start at the bottom again and work up. Fourteenth Street is still the Mecca of this type of salesmen; thirty-eight were recently counted between Sixth Avenue and Union Square and at one point there was a cluster of five.

Unemployment has brought back the newsboy in increasing numbers. He avoids the busy corners, where news stands are frequent, and hawks his papers in the side streets with surprising success. His best client is the man who is "too tired to walk down to the corner for a paper."

Selling Sunday papers has become a science. Youngsters have found that it is extremely profitable to invade apartment houses between 11 and 12 o'clock Sunday morning, knock on each apartment door, and offer the Sunday editions. Their profits are usually between $1.50 and $2.

IV

A HUNGRY CROWD RAIDS A STORE

During the first years of the depression many descriptions of hunger riots were published. The following newspaper account is typical. □ "Food Rioters Raid Oklahoma City Store; 500 Dispersed by the Police With Tear Gas." *The New York Times,* January 21, 1931, p. 1. Copyright © 1931 by The New York Times Company. Reprinted by permission.

OKLAHOMA CITY, Jan. 20 (AP).—A crowd of men and women, shouting that they were hungry and jobless, raided a grocery store near the City Hall today. Twenty-six of the men were arrested. Scores loitered near the city jail following the arrests, but kept well out of range of fire hose made ready for use in case of another disturbance.

The police tonight broke up a second meeting of about one hundred unemployed men and arrested Francis Owens, alleged head of the "Oklahoma City Unemployed Council," who was accused of instigating the raid.

Before the grocery was entered, a delegation of unemployed, led by Owens, had demanded of City Manager E. M. Fry that the authorities furnish immediate relief. Owens rejected a request by Mr. Fry for the names and addresses of the "Unemployed Council," said to number 2,500 men and women, both whites and Negroes.

The raiders disregarded efforts of H. A. Shaw, the store manager, to quiet them. "It is too late to bargain with us," the leaders shouted, as they stripped the shelves.

The police hastily assembled emergency squads and dispersed the crowd numbering 500, with tear gas. Only those who were trapped in the wrecked store were arrested. Five women among them were released. The windows of the store were smashed as the raiders attempted to flee.

John Simmons was held on a charge of assault after he had leaped on the back of Lee Mullenix, a policeman, when the officer attempted to enter the crowded store.

Floyd Phillips was charged with inciting a riot. The police said he was one of the speakers who harangued the crowd at the City Hall before they began the parade that ended at the store.

V

LIVES OF THE UNEMPLOYED

By 1932 millions of Americans were on relief, and the money to keep them from starvation was running out. The following testimony given by a social worker before a Senate committee in May 1932 indicates the dimensions of the problem. □ *Federal Cooperation in Unemployment Relief,* Hearing before a Subcommittee of the Committee on Manufactures, United States Senate, 72nd Congress, 1st Session, on S.4592. Washington, D.C.: United States Congress, 1932.

The next witness is Mr. Karl de Schweinitz, who is executive secretary of the Community Council of Philadelphia, and also secretary of the committee on unemployment relief.

MR. DE SCHWEINITZ. When I appeared before the Subcommittee of the Committee on Manufactures last December [1931], I stated that there were

238,000 persons out of work in Philadelphia and that we estimated unemployment in the city in ordinary times to be between 40,000 and 50,000. There are now 298,000 persons out of work. In other words, whereas in December our unemployment was a little less than five times what one might call normal unemployment, to-day it is six times normal unemployment.

In December I told you that 43,000 families were receiving relief. To-day 55,000 families are receiving relief.

In December our per family grant was $4.39 per week per family. It is now $4.23 per family. Of this $4.23 per family, about $3.93 is an allowance for food. This is about two-thirds of the amount needed to provide a health-maintaining diet.

When I was here in December you asked me how long our funds would last. I said that I thought they would last into May. They lasted only until April 11. We are now using funds secured through the Talbot bill,[1] which has already been referred to. We hope that the money will carry us some time into the latter part of June. Our private resources are exhausted.

SENATOR WAGNER. What will you do then?

MR. DE SCHWEINITZ. I do not know. We are trying to induce the State legislature to hold a special session. That is our only hope. There is absolutely no possibility in the immediate future of securing any more money from private sources.

When I was here in December we had available in Philadelphia a little upwards of $4,600,000 from privately collected funds. This is the money which has been expended. Our only hope now is in governmental relief. I see no chance before next fall of getting any additional money through private contributions.

SENATOR COSTIGAN. Do you refer to Federal aid?

MR. DE SCHWEINITZ. Federal and State. I think there is very little chance of any money being available now from the city of Philadelphia.

I think you are interested in knowing about things that apply all over the country, and starvation has no geographical boundaries. Starvation in Philadelphia is just as true for New Mexico as it is for South Dakota or any other place.

I want to emphasize two or three things. First of all I want to repeat what I said before that our grant for food is $3.93 a week and that it is only about two-thirds adequate. Then I want to tell you about an experi-

---

[1] A bill making $10,000,000 available for relief purposes in the state. Welfare workers reported that 250,000 families were receiving relief in Pennsylvania and "that anything short of $60,000,000 to $70,000,000 would not even provide food."—*Editors.*

ence we had in Philadelphia when our private funds were exhausted and before public funds became available.

On April 11 we mailed to families the last food orders which they received from private funds. It was not until April 22 that the giving of aid to families from public funds began, so that there was a period of about 11 days when many families received nothing. We have received reports from workers as to how these families managed. The material I am about to give you is typical, although it is based on a small sample. We made an intensive study of 91 families to find out what happened when the food orders stopped.

In a little less than 9 per cent of these families there were pregnant mothers and in a little more than one-third of the families children of nursing age.

This is how some of these families managed.

One woman said she borrowed 50 cents from a friend and bought stale bread for 3½ cents per loaf, and that is all they had for eleven days except for one or two meals.

With the last food order another woman received she bought dried vegetables and canned goods. With this she made a soup and whenever the members of the family felt hungry they just ate some of the soup. . . .

One woman went along the docks and picked up vegetables that fell from the wagons. Sometimes the fish vendors gave her fish at the end of the day. On two different occasions this family was without food for a day and a half.

One family had nothing the day the food order stopped until 9 o'clock at night. Then the mother went to a friend's house and begged for a loaf of bread. This woman finally got two days' work at 75 cents a day. She bought a little meat and made a stew from vegetables picked up which they cooked over again every day to prevent its spoiling.

Another family's food consisted of potatoes, rice, bread, and coffee, and for a period of a day and a half they had no food at all.

SENATOR COSTIGAN. Are the cases you are citing typical or extreme?

MR. DE SCHWEINITZ. They are typical. I could tell you about many others, but while tragic it would become monotonous, and a few will illustrate the situation as well as many. . . .

I should also like to say that when we talk to people who ask about unemployment they say, "Well, people manage to get along somehow or other, don't they? You do not have very many people who really drop dead of starvation." That is perfectly true. Actually, death from starvation is not a frequent occurrence. You do not often hear about casualties of that sort. This is because people live in just the way I have described. They live on inadequacies, and because they live on inadequacies the thing does not become dramatic and we do not hear about it. Yet the cost in human suffering is just as great as if they starved to death overnight. . . .

SENATOR CUTTING. You do not think the unfortunate recipients would feel more demoralized than they do if they felt the aid was coming from Federal sources rather than from local sources?

MR. DE SCHWEINITZ. I think the real demoralization is not relief, it is unemployment. What really hurts people is being out of their jobs. Think of what work means to each one of us. It is just exactly the same with the man in the ditch. People like their work. When they have a day off they time and time again will visit their working place. It is the loss of employment that is demoralizing, getting out of the habit of work. Once you take that away from a man you have done the damage. As far as Federal or State aid goes, it does not make any difference.

PROBLEM **14**

Government and the Economy During the 1930's

The decade from 1929 to 1939 marked the low point in American economic history and the most prolonged depression ever encountered in the United States. During this decade human suffering was greater, more farms were foreclosed, more banks closed their doors, and more unemployed men stalked the streets of American cities than in any ten-year period before or since. And more measures were taken to end the depression and to prevent its recurrence than anyone in 1929 imagined.

The depression also marked the end in American economic history of a belief in a self-regulating economic system. Raised on the maxims of Adam Smith, an eighteenth-century economist and advocate of laissez-faire capitalism, men in pre-depression days had argued that the economy would right itself if the government would only let it alone. But as the economy sank deeper into the depression and as men of every walk of life faced ruin, a resounding cry for government intervention reached the ears of the lawmakers. The result was the New Deal.

The New Deal was a pragmatic and disjointed attempt to meet the crisis of the depression through a host of legislative acts related to one another in only the loosest sort of way. The science of economic forecasting was in its infancy in 1932. John Maynard Keynes, the British economist who became the prophet of the new economics, did not publish his famous book, *The General Theory of Employment, Interest, and Money,* until 1936. Within the New Deal several schools of thought competed for the attention of President Franklin D. Roosevelt. Moreover, many of the men who besieged FDR could not claim to belong to any school of thought at all. They were advocates of this policy or that policy, directed toward solving a specific problem, whether or not the solution fit into an overall economic scheme.

While the New Dealers have been condemned for planning too much, they can more justly be accused of planning too little. Yet the reforms they made produced a lasting effect upon the American economy. The measures to regulate the stock market made speculation on the scale of the big bull market impossible. The banking reforms made bank failures a national rarity. Legislation to provide such benefits as unemployment compensation, social security, and minimum wage laws built automatic stabilizers into the economy to temper the ups and downs of the business cycle. The Employment Act of 1946, passed in the spirit of the New Dealers, placed responsibility for overseeing the health of the economy squarely in the hands of the federal government.

The authors of the reading in Problem 14 discuss some of these matters and raise important questions about the entire depression decade. As you read, think about the following questions:

1   Have the authors satisfactorily revealed why the depression lasted so long?

2   The authors believe that, during a depression, government should spend more money than it collects in taxes. Did the New Dealers follow this policy?

3   What permanent changes in the relationship of the government and the economic system were made during the New Deal?

4   How far apart were Hoover and Roosevelt in their approach to ending the depression?

A CURE FOR THE DEPRESSION

In the following article, the authors discuss the policies of Hoover and Roosevelt and suggest that the depression could have been cured with corrective legislation. Whether their theory would have worked will remain unknown. World War II began when the economy was still at a low point. With the war came increased industrial activity, a stimulus to agriculture, and rising prices. Burck and Silberman, editors of *Fortune* Magazine, credit the New Dealers with the reforms which led to a relatively stable and prosperous economy.

☐ Gilbert Burck and Charles E. Silberman, "Why the Depression Lasted So Long," pp. 85, 189, 190, 192, 194, 196, 199, 200. Reprinted from the March 1955 issue of *Fortune* Magazine by special permission; copyright © 1955 Time Inc.

The basic reason the depression lasted so long was, of course, the economic ignorance of the times. Economics is one of the most elusive subjects that has ever engaged the intelligence of man, and economics has never been more baffling or elusive than it was in the 1930's. Venerable economic principles, the principles on which industrial civilization was erected, were suddenly powerless to account and prescribe for what was happening. All that most experts understood was that something new was happening, and it was years before they knew just what to make of it.

Neither Herbert Hoover nor Franklin Roosevelt, alas, knew what to make of it. Herbert Hoover . . . would not desert his convictions on the inviolability of the gold standard and the balanced budget . . . . Roosevelt . . . unhesitatingly and even gaily threw over laissez faire and embraced a managed economy. But he, too, was haunted by the ideal of a balanced budget, and his deficits were too small to counteract the decline in private spending. And in 1936 he lost his nerve and practically balanced the 1937 budget—with disastrous results. . . .

. . . Contrary . . . to popular myth, Hoover's economics were not incorrigibly laissez faire. Many of his associates, particularly Andrew Mellon, urged him to let things alone . . . . But Hoover pointed out that the vast majority of Americans no longer lived and worked on the land, and no longer could sit out a depression on the farm; the depression meant heavy unemployment in the cities, and untold and unprecedented suffering. So he had announced late in 1929 that recovery was the government's responsibility. In 1930–32 he actually introduced many of the important measures that later became the bases of Roosevelt's recovery program. Through RFC [Reconstruction Finance Corporation] he supplemented private credit for business with government credit. He created a little employment through public works. He plugged for high wage rates. He tried to cope with farm surpluses by withholding them from the market. And he tried to expand credit.

Having done all this, however, Hoover stuck doggedly not only to the gold standard but also to the balanced budget . . . . [He believed that their] abandonment under any circumstances was something that could be seriously considered only by knaves, collectivists, or crackpots. . . . Although Hoover ran deficits in 1931 and 1932, these were largely involuntary. And it was to balance the budget that he persuaded the American Legion to forgo demanding a bonus, vetoed a direct relief bill, and took a resolute stand against "squandering the nation into prosperity."

To be sure, practically everybody in 1931 and 1932 thought as Hoover did—including Franklin Roosevelt. Practically nobody understood what today is commonly understood—that a deficit, if it occurs when a nation's resources and labor forces are only partly utilized, need not be inflationary. Although John Maynard Keynes was already arguing in the press that deficit financing could cure the depression, it was not till 1936 that he launched the "Keynesian Revolution" with his *General Theory of Employment, Interest, and Money,* which, among other things, popularized the notion that a government's finances should be managed primarily in terms of their effect on the economy's stability.

Another and less academic partisan of deficit spending was a then obscure Utah banker named Marriner Eccles, who had never read Keynes. What the government should do, he told his scandalized banker friends, was not merely to loosen credit, not merely to devalue, but to spend more than it took in, in order to increase the nation's buying power.[1] The government of 1930–32, he argued, was 'like the stewards on the doomed *Titanic,* who locked all the staterooms so that nothing could be stolen as the ship sank.

Taking everything together, history may well agree with the verdicts of Walter Lippmann and the late A. D. Gayer, the Columbia University monetary economist. Professor Gayer argued that Hoover's inconsistency was disastrous, that either he should have followed Andrew Mellon's formula and let deflation take its natural, brutal course, . . . or he should have supported employment and personal income directly besides shoring up banks, insurance companies, and railroads. He succeeded only in prolonging the decline without mitigating it very much. As for Lippmann, he argued in the 1930's that the one real difference between the Hoover and Roosevelt administrations was the former's refusal to abandon the gold standard, and that the Hoover Administration crucified itself on a cross of gold.

By the close of 1932 the whole nation had been pretty well crucified on the same cross. Industrial production stood at only 50 per cent of its mid-1929 level, and gross national product had fallen 40 per cent, to $67 billion (1929 dollars). Nearly 13 million men—some estimates ran to 15 million or 16 million—were out of work, not counting several million more on short weeks. Wages and salaries had fallen 40 per cent.

---

[1] Later on, as Federal Reserve governor, Eccles also argued consistently enough that in inflationary times the government should reduce the nation's buying power by running a surplus. —*Gilbert Burck and Charles E. Silberman.*

Since people always stop buying postponable things first, the worst decline was suffered by the durable-goods business, which had boomed early in the 1920's.

Unlike the volume of non-durables and services, which in real terms declined no more than 15 per cent, that of durable consumer goods dropped 50 per cent. Auto production fell from 4,000,000 in 1929 to 1,100,000 in 1932. Residential construction withered away to less than 25 per cent of its 1929 volume; only 134,000 new nonfarm units were started in 1932, compared to 509,000 in 1929, and 937,000 in 1925, at the peak of the residential boom. Because corporations (taken together) lost $2 billion in 1932 and again in 1933, and because excess capacity was depressing prices in almost every industry, business cut its purchases of capital equipment (producer durables) by 50 per cent, and cut industrial and commercial construction 70 per cent.

Meantime, the financial crisis grew more acute. The Dow-Jones average dropped to 40, mortgage foreclosures rose sharply, and bank failures mounted. In the first two months of 1933 hoarding increased by $900 million, and the merest rumor was enough to start a run on a bank. Farm-mortgage riots spread all over the Midwest as farmers took over foreclosure sales and forced the resale of foreclosed properties to mortgagees for a few dollars. . . .

When Roosevelt took office his advisers were full of ideas, many conflicting, about what had gone wrong—the nation's capital stock had been overexpanded, prices had been "managed," labor hadn't got a fair share of income, public utilities had been antisocial, and so on. But at first Roosevelt and his Administration had one important broad, fixed objective: to raise production by stimulating purchasing power, and to achieve this objective they were willing to try anything plausible. In a press conference Roosevelt compared himself to a football quarterback who can call only one play at a time, and must decide each play on the basis of how the previous one worked.

This pragmatic, experimental approach was perhaps the only intelligent one in those early days of the New Deal, and for a time it worked very well. Roosevelt's cheerful ignorance of economics, far from being a handicap, was if anything an advantage, for it made him receptive to the new and unorthodox. The trouble came later on, when it became necessary to stop improvising and choose a sound approach to the nation's problems and stick to it.

But the earliest measures of the new Administration, in March, 1933, were consistent enough. In his 1932 campaign Roosevelt had, much to his later embarrassment, argued eloquently against an unbalanced budget. "Stop the deficits," he had implored. "I accuse the Administration of being the biggest spending Administration in peacetimes in all our history." And the first thing the New Deal had to do, after reopening the solvent banks, was to "restore confidence" by demonstrating that it could cut expenditures and balance the budget. An economy act was passed, and federal salaries and other costs were cut. What would have happened if this deflationary course had been followed to the bitter end is hard to say, but even most businessmen by this time were afraid to let it happen.

At all events, the Administration reversed itself and moved rapidly toward credit expansion, monetary inflation, price and wage rises, relief payments, and public works. The most important decision was to go off gold, and the decision was in effect forced on Roosevelt by an inflation-minded Congress. On April 20, 1933, Roosevelt placed an embargo on gold, and thus in effect took the country off the gold standard.

There followed, between 1933 and 1937, a continuous avalanche of congressional acts and executive orders dealing with recovery. There were steps primarily designed to raise prices and boost purchasing power—though some of them involved various reforms. There was, of course, pump priming by means of a bewildering succession of public works and relief measures. There was the Federal Emergency Relief Administration, the Civilian Conservation Corps, the Civil Works Administration, and PWA [Public Works Administration], which under "Honest" Harold Ickes spent so little money that WPA [Works Projects Administration] had to be formed under Harry Hopkins. Partly as a result of these measures federal expenditures rose from $3.7 billion in 1932 to $8.2 billion in 1936 (in 1929 dollars).

There was TVA [Tennessee Valley Authority], which got the government into the power business in a colossal way. There were aids to agriculture like "parity" prices and the AAA [Agricultural Adjustment Administration], which raised prices by paying farmers to restrict production. There were several labor measures . . . which raised union membership from about two million in 1932 to over 11 million in 1941. There were a variety of measures easing home and farm mortgages. And there was the social-security system, founded in 1936.

Among the solidest early achievements of the New Deal were the laws reforming and strengthening the banking system, such as the Banking Act of 1933, which provided for deposit insurance and for the divorce of investment and commercial banking; the Banking Act of 1935, which centralized Federal Reserve power, particularly over open-market operations; and the Securities and Exchange Acts of 1934–35, which reformed the issuing and buying and selling of securities.

Sidney Weinberg [an investment banker], who fought hard against the Securities and Exchange Acts, now [1955] says he would go on a crusade against any move to repeal them. And Professor Milton Friedman of the University of Chicago, one of the leading orthodox economists, argues that the Federal Deposit Insurance Corporation is by all odds the most important of the changes affecting the cyclical characteristics of the American economy, perhaps even more important than the establishment of the Federal Reserve.

For all their inconsistencies, the New Deal's early measures did achieve their major aim: they raised farm and industrial prices and wages, and so stimulated consumption and industrial production. Gross national product . . . rose just about as fast as it had declined, and by the third quarter of 1937 stood 5 per cent above its mid-1929 level. Industrial production had also passed the 1929 peak, and volume of consumer non-durables was 10 per cent above 1929. This, however, was not full recovery. Because the national working force had increased 10 per cent and its productivity 15 per cent, true recovery, that is, fairly full employment, would have meant a G.N.P. at least 25 per cent higher than in 1929. As it was, there were still more than seven million unemployed early in 1937.

What blocked full recovery, and so perpetuated mass unemployment, was the fact that the durables sector of the economy hardly recovered at all. By 1937 the volume of residential construction was still 40 per cent below its 1929 level, industrial and commercial construction . . . was 50 per cent below 1929, and producer and consumer durables were 5 and 6 per cent below 1929, respectively. Why did they lag?

The story of residential construction may be told simply. There had been considerable overbuilding in the 1920's, and the low incomes and low household formation of the Thirties created little additional demand. The birth rate fell 19 per cent, and people doubled up. And so long as lenders feared that new houses would have to compete with houses on which they had foreclosed, or held shaky mortgages, they were reluctant to give mortgages for new construction. Then, too, building costs did not fall so much as costs in general.

The stagnation in capital spending—on industrial and commercial construction and producers' goods—is not so simple a story. The volume of commercial construction was so great in 1929 that it was not equaled again until 1954; thus the overbuilding and speculative real-estate inflation of the 1920's were among the main reasons why 1937's volume remained only half of the 1929's volume. Then, too, commercial construction is closely related to the rate of home building, which was low.

Even the fact that the 1937 volume of producers' goods was only 5 per cent below its 1929 volume was disappointing. . . . And why did not this capital spending on equipment and plant recover? . . .

One answer popular in the late 1930's was . . . [the] theory of secular stagnation, which blamed oversaving at a time when investment opportunities were declining, thanks to the economy's "maturity." What seems today a more plausible reason is that business probably was not able to adjust to all the changes that confronted it in a few short years:

The reform of the credit system, as well as SEC [Securities and Exchange Commission] regulations, were badly needed, but probably discouraged new-issue flotation.

Legalized unionization elevated wage rates 41 per cent in 1933–37. Even harder to accept, for many businessmen, was that unions had to be recognized and bargained with.

Increasingly higher taxes altered the calculations on which investments had been based. In his attempts to balance the budget, Hoover had raised tax *rates* drastically in 1932. The New Deal raised them further, and added new taxes—e.g., excess-profits taxes, social-security taxes, and the undistributed-profits tax. It had also closed many loopholes, such as personal holding companies. As business and income picked up, therefore, tax payments rose even more. Federal receipts more than tripled between 1932 and 1937, rising (in 1929 dollars) from $2 billion to $6.8 billion, or nearly double the 1929 figure of $3.8 billion.

Banking regulations, unionization, and higher taxes, of course, are commonplace enough today. But the speed with which business had to adjust to them had a lot to do with its reluctance to make capital investment. Its adjustment problems were not eased by the increasingly uncompromising attitude of President Roosevelt. He had provocation, it is true. Some businessmen were venting a virtually psychopathic hatred of "that man." Roosevelt went on to assume that all businessmen, save a few New Deal "captives," were enemies of the people. His 1936 message to Congress was studded with such fighting phrases as "entrenched greed" and "resplendent economic autocracy," and his campaign speeches were even less conciliatory. . . .

Yet there remains one other important circumstance that probably contributed greatly to the lag in capital goods. What really shapes business decisions to buy capital goods is not a vague sense of confidence or doubt, not necessarily even an inflationary or deflationary government policy, but the outlook for sales and profits. Partly because of rising wages, partly because of rising taxes (and partly because 1929 profits were unusually high), profits in the 1930's did not recover so fast as wages and production. Corporate profits in 1937, after taxes, were 43 per cent below their 1929 level, and the sales outlook for the durable industries was still bad. But could anything have been done about *that?* The government could have kept taxes down by running somewhat bigger deficits. And why didn't this high-spending government run bigger deficits? Simply because Roosevelt was constantly plagued by the ideal of a balanced budget and by congressional advocates of sound money, and never seemed to understand quite how an unbalanced budget need not be inflationary (though he actually needed some inflation). Thus is irony defined. . . .

For all its fumbling and faulty signal calling, the New Deal passed on to the post war generation a heritage of reforms and practices without which today's economy would not be nearly so strong and well balanced as it is. Aside from social security and financial reforms, the most important features of the heritage are the practices that enable our economy to remain a market economy despite big business, big unions, and big government, which have no place in a classic market economy of many small suppliers, each without significant control over the market.

Labor's right to organize its own unions and bargain collectively, for example, may give labor what sometimes amounts to monopoly power, but a vigorous labor movement helps solve the major problem of an economy whose output is increasing much faster than its population: how to distribute the benefits of rising productivity as fast as they are created.

Another important legacy of the great depression is an expanded understanding of how delicately a big economy is balanced, and the extent to which the government can or cannot effectively check imbalances before they grow serious. What with the growth in the government's fact-finding activities, the imbalances of the kind that eventually ruined the economy of the 1920's could not today [1955] go unnoticed, and it is unlikely that they could go uncorrected.

Today, at all events, we have the spectacle of a Republican Administration talking in a way that not merely would have astonished Calvin Coolidge, but in its calm assertion of responsibility in a relatively minor swing of the business cycle might have given pause even to Franklin Roosevelt. "Definite and deliberate steps were taken to promote a stable prosperity," Dwight Eisenhower told Congress . . . in discussing the 1953–54 recession (in his annual Economic Report). The steps included a reversal of the Administration's hard-money policy and an unhesitating if temporary abandonment of its attempts to balance the budget. Together with "automatic" stabilizers like unemployment insurance and reduced tax payments, these steps more than offset a $4.4-billion decline in income derived from manufacturing, and gave people $1 billion more to spend than the year before. Says the report: "This remarkable result—namely, a rise in disposable personal income accompanying a 10 per cent decline in industrial production—has no parallel in our recorded economic history."

But all the depression-generated reforms and practices were not realized without a price. They encouraged a general idea that if a little government is a good thing, a lot of government is that much better. Specifically, they encouraged a belief that only continually *expanding* government expenditures and deficits can sustain prosperity. They encouraged those thinkers who solemnly proposed to cure the abuses of private monopolies by replacing them with government monopolies. They were, of course, a godsend to many politicians and bureaucrats. And the trend toward bigger government was strengthened by World War II, when the government had to control prices, allocate materials, and ration goods and manpower.

The inevitable reaction, both at home and abroad, set in shortly after World War II, when the much-heralded postwar crash never came, when in fact inflation turned out to be the great problem. There was a general realization that a market that is imperfect by strict classical standards is vastly better than none at all, that competition does work, that inflation in prosperous times is an evil less reprehensible only than dogmatic liquidation when millions are unemployed, that business and the businessman are worth a new vote of confidence.

This reaction, however, is not merely a pendulum's swing back to the 1920's and the decadent laissez faire Stuart Chase [an American economist and writer] described so indignantly.

The reaction may be best described in terms of Hegel's opposing thesis and antithesis, out of which a new synthesis is born. In his last Economic Report, President Eisenhower tried to indicate its direction. Discussing the doctrinaire manifestations of the old and the new positions, he described one as insensitive to the misfortunes of depression, the other to the inequities of inflation. "Each carries the danger of undermining, sooner or later, our system of free competitive enterprise . . . The need of our times is for economic policies that recognize the proven success of sustained economic growth and betterment . . . and respect the need of people for a sense of security as well as opportunity." Such is the tendency of the New Economy, which if wisely guided can accelerate the astonishing progress that has enabled the material well-being of Americans to advance more in the past fifty years than the material well-being of the human race has advanced in all the previous centuries of Western history.

PROBLEM **15**

The Great Depression: An Interpretation

Debates about the cause of the Great Depression broke out almost as soon as news of the stock market crash reached the newspapers. The debate has never slackened. In recent years it has focused on three questions. What caused the depression to begin in 1929 instead of in some other year? What caused the depression to be so severe? And why did the depression last for such a long period? Problems 10 through 14 have touched on each of these three issues, and in Problem 15 John Kenneth Galbraith concentrates on the conditions in 1929 that led to the depression.

The depression itself was responsible for a renewed interest in the business cycle among historians and economists. As they perfected their research methods, they made them more and more complex until the layman had great difficulty understanding the issues. Still the basic ideas which have emerged from this research are not difficult to understand once a student has a grasp of the evidence.

The interpretation of the Great Depression has been overlaid with partisan political controversy. In the 1930's particularly, many articles and books about this great national disaster turned out to be disguised defenses of, or attacks on, the major party leaders, particularly Hoover and Roosevelt. Since the end of World War II, the partisan nature of the controversy has diminished, and the era can be viewed with greater detachment than it could when the long bread lines wound around street corners or when farmers saw their family holdings sold beneath the auctioneer's hammer.

Problem 15 is taken from J. Kenneth Galbraith's book *The Great Crash, 1929,* an analysis of the depression written by a professional economist for the general public. Although he avoids the technical language of the learned journals, Professor Galbraith takes up the issues which have long separated economic historians. As you read, think about the following questions:

1   Why did the depression begin in 1929?

2   What could anyone have done about the elements which caused the depression? What steps, if any, could the federal government have taken to help prevent it?

3   Does Galbraith feel that the economic experts should have been able to foresee the disaster?

4   How was the crash in October 1929 related to the depression which followed it?

5   Of the five weaknesses in the economy mentioned by Galbraith in the reading, which weaknesses are the most closely related?

THE CRASH AND THE DEPRESSION

J. Kenneth Galbraith, professor of economics at Harvard and former ambassador to India, wrote this analysis of the relationship of the stock market crash to the depression. ☐ John Kenneth Galbraith, *The Great Crash, 1929,* pp. 179–186, 187–188, 190–193. Boston: Houghton Mifflin Company, copyright © 1955.

What, then, are the plausible causes of the depression? The task of answering can be simplified somewhat by dividing the problem into two parts. First there is the question of why economic activity turned down in 1929. Second there is the vastly more important question of why, having started down, on this unhappy occasion it went down and down and down and remained low for a full decade.

As noted, the Federal Reserve indexes of industrial activity and of factory production, the most comprehensive monthly measures of economic activity then available, reached a peak in June [1929]. They then turned down and continued to decline throughout the rest of the year. The turning point in other indicators—factory payrolls, freight-car loadings, and department store sales—came later, and it was October or after before the trend in all of them was clearly down. Still, as economists have generally insisted, and the matter has the high authority of the National Bureau of Economic Research, the economy had weakened in the early summer well before the crash.

This weakening can be variously explained. Production of industrial products, for the moment, had outrun consumer and investment demand for them. The most likely reason is that business concerns, in the characteristic enthusiasm of good times, misjudged the prospective increase in demand and acquired larger inventories than they later found they needed. As a result they curtailed their buying, and this led to a cutback in production. In short, the summer of 1929 marked the beginning of the familiar inventory recession. The proof is not conclusive from (by present standards) limited figures available. Department store inventories, for which figures are available, seem not to have been out of line early in the year. But a mild slump in department store sales in April could have been a signal for curtailment.

Also there is a chance—one that students of the period have generally favored—that more deep-seated factors were at work and made themselves seriously evident for the first time during that summer. Throughout the twenties production and productivity per worker grew steadily: between 1919 and 1929, output per worker in manufacturing industries increased by about 43 per cent. Wages, salaries, and prices all remained comparatively stable, or in any case underwent no comparable increase. Accordingly, costs fell and with prices the same, profits increased. These profits sustained the spending of the well-to-do, and they also nourished at least some of the expectations behind the stock market boom. Most of all they encouraged a very high level of capital investment. During the twenties, the production of capital goods increased at an average annual rate of 6.4 per cent a year; non-durable consumers' goods, a category which includes such objects of mass consumption as food and clothing, increased at a rate of only 2.8 per cent. (The rate of increase for durable consumers' goods such as cars, dwellings, home furnishings, and the like, much of it representing expenditures of the well-off to well-to-do, was 5.9 per cent.) A large and increasing investment in capital goods was, in other words, a principal device by which the profits were being spent. It follows that anything that interrupted the investment outlays—anything, indeed, which kept them from showing the necessary rate of increase—could cause trouble. When this occurred, compensation through an increase in consumer spending could not automatically be expected. The effect, therefore, of insufficient investment—investment that failed to keep pace with the steady increase in profits—could be falling total demand reflected . . . in falling orders and output. Again there is no final proof of this point, for unfortunately we do not know how rapidly investment had to grow to keep abreast of the current increase in profits. However, the explanation is broadly consistent with the facts.

There are other possible explanations of the downturn. Back of the insufficient advance in investment may have been the high interest rates. Perhaps, although less probably, trouble was transmitted to the economy as a whole from some weak sector like agriculture. Further explanations could be offered. But one thing about this experience is clear. Until well along in the autumn of 1929 the downturn was limited. The recession in business activity was modest and underemployment relatively slight. Up to November it was possible to argue that not much of anything had happened. On other occasions, as noted—in 1924 and 1927 and of late in 1949—the economy has undergone similar recession. But, unlike these other occasions, in 1929 the recession continued and continued and got violently worse. This is the unique feature of the 1929 experience. This is what we need really to understand.

There seems little question that in 1929, modifying a famous cliché, the economy was fundamentally unsound. This is a circumstance of first-rate importance. Many things were wrong, but five weaknesses seem to have had an especially intimate bearing on the ensuing disaster. They are:

1) The bad distribution of income. In 1929 the rich were indubitably rich. The figures are not entirely satisfactory, but it seems certain that the 5 per cent of the population with the highest incomes in that year received approximately one third of all personal income. The proportion of personal income received in the form of interest, dividends, and rent—the income, broadly speaking, of the well-to-do—was about twice as great as in the years following the Second World War.

This highly unequal income distribution meant that the economy was dependent on a high level of investment or a high level of luxury consumer spending or both. The rich cannot buy great quantities of bread. If they are to dispose of what they receive it must be on luxuries or by way of investment in new plants and new projects. Both investment and luxury spending are subject, inevitably, to more erratic influences and to wider fluctuations than the bread and rent outlays of the $25-a-week workman. This high-bracket spending and investment was especially susceptible, one may assume, to the crushing news from the stock market in October of 1929.

2) The bad corporate structure. In November 1929, a few weeks after the crash, the Harvard Economic Society gave as a principal reason why a depression need not be feared its reasoned judgment that "business in most lines has been conducted with prudence and conservatism." The fact was that American enterprise in the twenties had opened its hospitable arms to an

exceptional number of promoters, grafters, swindlers, impostors, and frauds. This, in the long history of such activities, was a kind of flood tide of corporate larceny.

The most important corporate weakness was inherent in the vast new structure of holding companies and investment trusts. [A holding company does not produce goods. It buys, or holds, the stocks of other companies which do produce goods.] The holding companies controlled large segments of the utility, railroad, and entertainment business. Here, as with the investment trusts, was the constant danger of devastation by reverse leverage. In particular, dividends from the operating companies paid the interest on the bonds of upstream holding companies. The interruption of the dividends meant default on the bonds, bankruptcy, and the collapse of the structure. Under these circumstances, the temptation to curtail investment in operating plant in order to continue dividends was obviously strong. This added to deflationary pressures. The latter, in turn, curtailed earnings and helped bring down the corporate pyramids. When this happened, even more retrenchment was inevitable. Income was earmarked for debt repayment. Borrowing for new investment became impossible. It would be hard to imagine a corporate system better designed to continue and accentuate a deflationary spiral.

3) The bad banking structure. Since the early thirties, a generation of Americans has been told, sometimes with amusement, sometimes with indignation, often with outrage, of the banking practices of the late twenties. In fact, many of these practices were made ludicrous only by the depression. Loans which would have been perfectly good were made perfectly foolish by the collapse of the borrower's prices or the markets for his goods or the value of the collateral he had posted. The most responsible bankers—those who saw that their debtors were victims of circumstances far beyond their control and sought to help—were often made to look the worst. The bankers yielded, as did others, to the blithe, optimistic, and immoral mood of times but probably not more so. A depression such as that of 1929–32, were it to begin as this is written, would also be damaging to many currently impeccable banking reputations.

However, although the bankers were not unusually foolish in 1929, the banking structure was inherently weak. The weakness was implicit in the large numbers of independent units. When one bank failed, the assets of others were frozen while depositors elsewhere had a . . . warning to go and ask for their money. Thus one failure led to other failures, and these spread with a domino effect. Even in the best of times local misfortune or isolated mismanagement could start such a chain reaction. (In the first six months of 1929, 346 banks failed in various parts of the country with aggregate deposits of nearly $115 million.) When income, employment, and values fell as the result of a depression bank failures could quickly become epidemic. This happened after 1929. Again it would be hard to imagine a better arrangement for magnifying the effects of fear. The weak destroyed not only the other weak, but weakened the strong. People everywhere, rich and poor, were made aware of the disaster by the persuasive intelligence that their savings had been destroyed.

Needless to say, such a banking system, once in the convulsions of failure, had a uniquely repressive effect on the spending of its depositors and the investment of its clients.

4) The dubious state of the foreign balance. This is a familiar story. During the First World War, the United States became a creditor on international account. In the decade following, the surplus of exports over imports which once had paid the interest and principal on loans from Europe continued. The high tariffs, which restricted imports and helped to create this surplus of exports remained. However, history and traditional trading habits also accounted for the persistence of the favorable balance, so called.

Before, payments on interest and principal had in effect been deducted from the trade balance. Now that the United States was a creditor, they were added to this balance. The latter, it should be said, was not huge. In only one year (1928) did the excess of exports over imports come to as much as a billion dollars; in 1923 and 1926 it was only about $375,000,000. However, large or small, this difference had to be covered. Other countries which were buying more than they sold, and had debt payments to make in addition, had somehow to find the means for making up the deficit in their transactions with the United States.

During most of the twenties the difference was covered by cash—i.e., gold payments to the United States—and by new private loans by the United States to other countries. Most of the loans were to governments—national, state, or municipal bodies—and a large proportion were to Germany and Central and South America. The underwriters' margins in handling these loans were generous; the public took them up with enthusiasm; competition for the business was keen. If unfortunately corruption and bribery were required as competitive instruments, these were used. . . .

In all respects these operations were . . . a part of the New Era . . . . They were . . . fragile, and once the illusions of the New Era were dissipated they came . . . abruptly to an end. This, in turn, forced a fundamental revision in the foreign economic position of the United States. Countries could not cover their adverse trade balance with the United States with increased payments of gold, at least not for long. This meant that they had either to increase their exports to the United States or reduce their imports or default on their past loans.

President Hoover and the Congress moved promptly to eliminate the first possibility—that the accounts would be balanced by larger imports— by sharply increasing the tariff. Accordingly, debts, including war debts, went into default and there was a precipitate fall in American exports. The reduction was not vast in relation to total output of the American economy, but it contributed to the general distress and was especially hard on farmers.

5) The poor state of economic intelligence. To regard the people of any time as particularly obtuse seems vaguely improper, and it also establishes a precedent which members of this generation might regret. Yet it seems certain that the economists and those who offered economic counsel in the late twenties and early thirties were almost uniquely perverse. In the months and years following the stock market crash, the burden of reputable economic advice was invariably on the side of measures that would make things worse. In November of 1929, Mr. Hoover announced a cut in taxes; in the great no-business conferences that followed he asked business firms to keep up their capital investment and to maintain wages. Both of these measures were on the side of increasing spendable income, though unfortunately they were largely without effect. The tax reductions were negligible except in the higher income brackets; businessmen who promised to maintain investment and wages, in accordance with a well-understood convention, considered the promise binding only for the period within which it was not financially disadvantageous to do so. As a result investment outlays and wages were not reduced until circumstances would in any case have brought their reduction.

Still, the effort was in the right direction. Thereafter policy was almost entirely on the side of making things worse. Asked how the government could best advance recovery, the sound and responsible adviser urged that the budget be balanced. Both parties agreed on this. For Republicans the balanced budget was, as ever, high doctrine. But the Democratic Party platform of 1932, with an explicitness which politicians rarely advise, also called for a "federal budget annually balanced on the basis of accurate executive estimates within revenues . . ."

A commitment to a balanced budget is always comprehensive. It then meant there could be no increase in government outlays to expand purchasing power and relieve distress. It meant there could be no further tax reduction. But taken literally it meant much more. From 1930 on, the budget was far out of balance, and balance, therefore, meant an increase in taxes, a reduction in spending, or both. The Democratic platform in 1932 called for an "immediate and drastic reduction of governmental expenditures" to accomplish at least a 25 per cent decrease in the cost of government. . . .

The rejection of both fiscal (tax and expenditure) and monetary policy amounted precisely to a rejection of all affirmative government economic policy. The economic advisers of the day had both the unanimity and the authority to force the leaders of both parties to disavow all the available steps to check deflation and depression. In its own way this was a marked achievement—a triumph of dogma over thought. The consequences were profound.

It is in light of the above weaknesses of the economy that the role of the stock market crash in the great tragedy of the thirties must be seen. The years of self-depreciation by Wall Street to the contrary, the role is one of respectable importance. The collapse in securities values affected in the first instance the wealthy and the well-to-do. But we see that in the world of 1929 this was a vital group. The members disposed of a large proportion of the consumer income; they were the source of a lion's share of personal saving and investment. Anything that struck at the spending or investment by this group would of necessity have broad effects on expenditure and income in the economy at large. Precisely such a blow was struck by the stock market crash. In addition, the crash promptly removed from the economy the support that it had been deriving from the spending of stock market gains.

The stock market crash was also an exceptionally effective way of exploiting the weaknesses of the corporate structure. Operating companies at the end of the holding-company chain were forced by the crash to retrench. The subsequent collapse of these systems and also of the investment trusts effectively destroyed both the ability to borrow and the willingness to lend for investment. What have long looked like purely fiduciary effects were, in fact, quickly translated into declining orders and increasing unemployment.

The crash was also effective in bringing to an end the foreign lending by which the international accounts had been balanced. Now the accounts had, in the main, to be balanced by reduced exports. This put prompt and heavy pressure on export markets for wheat, cotton, and tobacco. Perhaps the foreign loans had only delayed an adjustment in the balance which had one day to come. The stock market crash served nonetheless to precipitate the adjustment with great suddenness at a most unpropitious time. The instinct of farmers who traced their troubles to the stock market was not totally misguided.

Finally, when the misfortune had struck, the attitudes of the time kept anything from being done about it. This, perhaps, was the most disconcerting feature of all. Some people were hungry in 1930 and 1931 and 1932. Others were tortured by the fear that they might go hungry. Yet others suffered the agony of the descent from the honor and respectability that goes with income into poverty. And still others feared that they would be next. Meanwhile everyone suffered from a sense of utter hopelessness. Nothing, it seemed, could be done. And given the ideas which controlled policy, nothing could be done.

Had the economy been fundamentally sound in 1929 the effect of the great stock market crash might have been small. Alternatively, the shock to confidence and the loss of spending by those who were caught in the market might soon have worn off. But business in 1929 was not sound; on the contrary it was exceedingly fragile. It was vulnerable to the kind of blow it received from Wall Street. Those who have emphasized this vulnerability are obviously on strong ground. Yet when a greenhouse succumbs to a hailstorm something more than a purely passive role is normally attributed to the storm. One must accord similar significance to the typhoon which blew out of lower Manhattan in October 1929.